CORE HUMILITY

A Story of Leadership Authenticity

by
Kevin Lavering

Contact:

http://authenturecoaching.com | klavering@gmail.com

Cover design and illustrations: Sarah Luce

ISBN: 979-8-9997063-0-0

Printed in the United States of America

First Edition

Table of Contents

Preface

Leadership is not simply a title—it's a journey of developing ourselves to strengthen others. It's a path marked by challenges, growth, rewards, and moments of deep self-reflection. This book was born not only from my own experiences—both the triumphs and the lessons—but also from the insights, stories, and wisdom generously shared by others along the way. Through these moments, I've come to believe that the most powerful form of leadership doesn't stem from authority or title, but from humility, authenticity, and generosity.

Over the years, I have seen great speakers and leaders who seem to connect well with others and have a positive influence on those around them. During these observations, a common thread emerged. Many of them led with a humble approach—one that resonated with people and created space for trust, growth, and genuine connection. More recently, I've been intentionally observing, researching, and reflecting on what helps someone become a humble leader. This book is the result of that exploration, crafted to share both the essence and a practical approach to what I call *Core Humility*.

My hope is that this book will serve as a guide, a mirror, and a source of encouragement for anyone seeking to lead with greater purpose and impact. It offers not just a story, but a practical methodology— an intentional approach to leadership grounded in humility. It invites you to explore a mindset and a set of practices that can shape how you show up, connect with others, and grow as a leader.

The story you're about to read follows Ryan Mitchell, a new leader stepping into a role filled with high expectations, uncertainty, and the quiet weight of self-doubt. While his journey is fictional, the challenges he faces are very real—ones that many of us have encountered in our own lives. Whether you're just beginning your leadership path or seeking a new perspective, you may see parts of yourself in Ryan's story: the pressure to prove yourself, the fear of not measuring up, and the desire to lead with confidence.

As Ryan's journey unfolds, he awakens to a new understanding of leadership—one not rooted in rank or appearance, but in being grounded in his authentic self. With the guidance of a mentor, he begins to recognize the subtle but powerful forces that often hold us back: impostor syndrome, the urge to compare, and a scarcity mindset. These challenges aren't merely professional hurdles; they are deeply human ones. And they're more common than we often admit.

As you read, I invite you to reflect on your own leadership experiences. Where have you struggled? When have you felt out of place or unsure? What leadership approaches seem to work for others but not for you? How can you connect more deeply with your team? Is there a better way—one that invites more trust, connection, and fulfillment? This book is not just about Ryan's journey—it's also about yours.

Whether you're stepping into leadership for the first time or seeking to enhance your influence, I invite you to explore these ideas with an open heart. May you find clarity, courage, and a renewed sense of calling in your own leadership journey.

I'm honored to share this journey with you.

— Kevin Lavering

Chapter 1: The Struggle

My office is quiet, but my thoughts are loud. I'm supposed to be a leader, yet here I am, staring at the walls of my new office, wrestling with a growing sense of inadequacy. I was filled with excitement and ambition when I accepted the position of Senior Manager of Project Management at FutureGen Power, a pioneering company at the forefront of modular nuclear generation. My office door proudly displays my name: Ryan Mitchell—Senior Manager. But as the clock ticks away on my very first day, self-doubt creeps in, whispering that perhaps I've bitten off more than I can chew.

So, how did I find myself in this whirlwind of uncertainty? Until recently, I was a lead engineer at FutureGen. Yet, a feeling of restlessness began to tug at me; I craved a new challenge that would push my limits. When the leadership opportunity arose, I seized it wholeheartedly. My extensive project experience and technical skills aligned well with this new role, and the allure of a higher salary, along with the prestige of increased responsibilities, was too enticing to resist. Now, here I sit, grappling with the weight of expectation, both from others and from myself, pondering if I truly have what it takes to rise to this occasion.

My friend and coworker, McKay, encouraged me to apply for this position on the project management team, believing that I had the right skills and mindset for the role. It felt like a natural next step in my career. Now, as I sit in my new office, I can't help but feel the weight of expectations pressing down on me.

Earlier in the day, as I logged into my computer, I felt a mix of anticipation and excitement. As my first official action as a new leader, I did what I had seen other great leaders do: I called a team meeting. Notifications fill my inbox one after another, which is encouraging; this could be a strong start. I remind myself that this meeting is my opportunity to set the tone and demonstrate that I belong here, despite the doubts echoing in my mind.

As I enter our conference room to meet my team, I'm immediately struck by the sudden hush that falls over the room. Conversations fade, and all eyes turn to me. The atmosphere is charged with curiosity and perhaps a hint of skepticism. Are they eager to meet their new leader, or are they simply sizing me up? Either way, I am determined not to let this moment slip away. My heart races as I realize I need to make a strong impression, and I want to do so confidently, even though I feel a bit out of my depth.

First on the agenda: introductions. Taking a deep breath, I sit at the table, aware of their attentive gazes. Coming from a different department, I understand the importance of establishing credibility. I share my background—my education, my experience in engineering—hoping each detail will help prove my qualifications to lead. "I'm looking forward to guiding our team to success and playing a pivotal role in each project," I say, trying to sound steady, but sensing a hint of rehearsed formality.

We go around the room, with each team member introducing themselves and updating me on their assignments and current challenges.

Sarah, a senior project manager, kicks things off. "I'm managing the Advanced Manufacturing Integration (AMI) project. Our main challenge is related to our testing—we're behind schedule by about a week."

A brief silence follows, the air thick with expectation. This is my cue. Even though testing isn't my area of expertise, I feel the urge to respond decisively. "We need to get this project back on track as soon as possible," I convey, summoning confidence. "Let's have the testing team work overtime to run the necessary test cases. I'll make sure management approves any additional pay."

To my surprise, Sarah's eyebrows lift in response. I take her silence as a win—this feels great.

Next, Sean, who oversees the Supply Chain Optimization (SCO) project, shares that his team has just overcome a significant hurdle by finalizing contract negotiations with their vendor.

"Sean, could you send me the final draft of the contract tomorrow? I'd like to take a look and give my feedback," I request, eager to be involved.

He hesitates for a moment, uncertainty on his face. "Uh… sure," he replies, though I can tell he's a bit taken aback. "Just so you know, all parties fully vetted this contract. We plan to sign it at the end of the week."

My heart quickens. A deadline looms, and I feel the pressure. If I back off now, I might appear unsure. "No problem. I'd still like to review that final draft tomorrow," I insist, striving to keep my voice steady.

Sean nods slowly, though I sense the tension in the room. He glances at Sarah, who looks equally apprehensive.

3

Then there's Aaron, our Organizational Change Management (OCM) lead. He assuredly states, "I have no challenges to report; everything is going smoothly." I catch Sarah and Sean exchanging glances, and a slight unease washes over me. "Aaron let's connect after the meeting," I suggest, trying to assert myself. "I'd like to go through your project in more detail."

Sarah quips lightly, "Aaron's in trouble, haha," shooting a glance at Sean.

That reaction catches me off guard—not quite the response I anticipated.

As the meeting progresses, I notice the energy in the room shifts. Updates become shorter and more cautious. By the time we wrap up, a weight settles over the room, and my team seems a bit worn. I had hoped to lead and inspire, but something just doesn't feel right.

Maybe it's first-day nerves. Perhaps they're not used to a leader who wants to be hands-on. Still, as I walk out of the meeting room, a flicker of uncertainty twists in my stomach. Am I really cut out for this?

———

As I mentioned earlier, here I am, staring at the walls of my new office, wrestling with a growing sense of inadequacy. It's still early on my first day in this position, and I'm already feeling this way. I need to bounce back quickly, but how?

After what felt like an hour of holding on to that thought and wondering what had gone wrong, Aaron walks in, laptop in hand. He takes a seat across from me at the conference table. He sets down his laptop and flips up the screen, feeling like a barrier between us. I try to sound upbeat, lifting my gaze. "I'm excited to work with our group and get involved in everyone's projects," I say, aiming for enthusiasm. "How can I support you?"

He nods, appreciating my intent, but I can't shake the feeling that he senses I'm still struggling to understand what true leadership really means. He turns his laptop around to show me a training module developed for Sarah's AMI project. As he explains the process of assessing the needs of end users and designing the training, I listen intently, nodding along while pretending I'm not over my head. This methodology is entirely new to me.

Our meeting wraps up, but I remain anchored in my chair, the weight of uncertainty still pressing on me, when Rachel, my new director and head of Manufacturing Operations, steps into my office.

"I'm looking forward to introducing you at my staff meeting today, Ryan," she says with a warm smile. "We'll see you at 1:00 p.m. in the conference room."

"Wonderful! Anything I need to prepare?" I ask, trying to sound composed.

"Nope, just bring yourself," she replies. "How's your first day going?"

"Great!" I answer quickly, but inside, I'm not so sure.

"I knew you were the right pick for this position," Rachel says. "See you in an hour."

"Can't wait," I reply, my voice thinner than I'd like.

———

I head to the cafeteria for lunch, feeling a bit hungry, and spot McKay in line for pizza by the slice. "Hey, McKay. Great to see you!" I call out, my voice cutting through the lunchtime chatter.

"Ryan! First day in the new role—how's the big office treating you?" he grins, and I can't help but grin back.

"It's going well," I say, half-joking as we move toward a quieter table. "And yes, I love the new office. It even has its own conference table for all my 'important' meetings," I add, trying to keep the mood light.

We find a table by the window and sit down, with the sun streaming in, creating a more relaxed atmosphere. After a few questions about my new role, the conversation shifts to our weekend plans. I casually mention my excitement about playing pickleball on Saturday and throw out the idea of McKay joining us. My uncle, Brian, has been coaching me, and he's eager to find a new teammate to liven up our matches. McKay jumps at the chance, promising to bring his A-game. This weekend is shaping up to be a fun blend of competition and camaraderie.

For the first time all day, I feel my shoulders relax. Talking with McKay feels easy, familiar—like I'm myself again. Not the version of me attempting to be a leader, but the real me. It's a stark contrast to the pressure I felt all morning. Why does this feel so natural, and everything else feels so forced? Am I trying too hard to follow someone else's script?

But as I head back to my desk, the urgency of the day hits me again. I ponder about the points I want to bring up during Rachel's staff meeting. I need to show I'm already making a positive impact. I need to prove I belong here. The confidence I felt during lunch with McKay starts to fade, replaced by that familiar knot of anxiety tightening inside me. It's time to focus; I can't let this chance slip away. I note the key accomplishments from my day. This should help demonstrate the value I'm bringing to the team:

Staff Meeting Notes:

- *Provide final review of the OptiChain software vendor contract*

- *Resolve the AMI project test delay*

- *New Idea—Set up weekly decision meetings with each of my reports (Decision Weeklies)*

As I walk into the conference room, I notice three other senior managers already seated. They quickly stand to greet me, shake my hand, and extend a warm welcome. Their friendliness catches me off guard. Rachel arrives shortly after, offering the same warm welcome. For a brief moment, I feel a surge of belonging. I'm part of the club now!

The meeting begins with company updates, moving swiftly to each manager sharing progress from their respective areas. I'm struck by something unexpected: they focus more on their teams' accomplishments than their own personal successes. They highlight collaboration, learning moments—even setbacks—with a kind of calm confidence that starts to intrigue me.

Mark, the senior manager of Quality, raises a significant concern during the meeting: his team is falling behind on testing their new Real-Time Root Cause Analysis (RTRCA) application. He takes full responsibility for the delay and expresses that the team is eager to utilize what they have learned.

Surprisingly, he is openly acknowledging the delay, and Rachel does not challenge him. Instead, she encourages him by saying, "I hope this will be a learning experience for your team that they can apply in the future. I look forward to your next progress update."

I can hardly believe what I'm witnessing. There is no defensiveness, no frantic attempts to appear in control. It's just honesty and a real sense of trust.

As the meeting progresses, Annie, the senior manager of Production Planning and Control, expresses her enthusiasm for the upcoming implementation of the OptiChain software. Sensing an opening to make my mark, I jump into the conversation.

"Yes, I plan to conduct a final review of that contract for Sean," I declare, attempting to project confidence.

Annie's expression shifts, a flicker of surprise crossing her face. "Oh—I thought we were ready for signatures. Sean did an excellent job gathering everyone's input and negotiating a strong agreement."

My heart sinks, a wave of panic washing over me. Did I just wade into territory that was already perfectly navigated by Sean?

"You're absolutely right," I reply hastily, trying to pivot back onto solid ground. "I'm certain Sean and the team put in magnificent work. My review will be quick."

"If you think it's necessary," Annie responds, her tone neutral yet supportive. She moves on, leaving me with a weight on my shoulders and the realization that my desire to contribute might have undermined the collaborative spirit we aim for.

Kristen, the senior manager of Process Improvement and Optimization, raises the issue of the delay in the AMI project. I sense the urgency and jump in again, hoping to make a better impact this time.

"I believe we'll have that under control soon," I assert. "I've instructed Sarah to have the testing team work overtime until we're back on schedule. She'll monitor progress and report to me regularly."

Kristen tilts her head, looking curious. "Is that really going to fix the issue? Sarah paused testing to investigate possible errors in the dataset. If the data's flawed, more testing could just waste time."

Another misstep. I didn't know that, and I felt exposed in front of this group.

Kristen finishes her update, and now it's my turn. I glance at my notes, my heart racing, anxious to find my place in this challenging environment and strive for a full recovery.

Staff Meeting Notes:

- *Provide final review of the OptiChain software vendor contract*
- *Resolve the AMI project test delay*

Great, I already covered those items. My list of today's accomplishments was getting pretty short. All that I had left on my list was a new idea, and that idea wasn't even something I had done yet:

- *New Idea—Set up weekly decision meetings with each of my reports (Decision Weeklies)*

My palms are sweaty as I share an idea I've been holding onto—something new I'd like to try in my one-on-one meetings with the team. As I speak, heads nod around the table. A flicker of relief washes over me. Thank goodness. Maybe I'm on the right track.

I continue, explaining that I plan to call these sessions "Decision Weeklies"—a space where each team member brings their weekly project decisions to me. The goal, I say, is to provide direction and maintain visibility across all projects.

But then I say it: "...so I can maintain a level of control over my team."

The word "control" hangs in the air longer than I expect. The room goes quiet. Eyebrows lift—not in admiration, but in caution. I feel the shift immediately. They're not impressed. They're concerned.

Rachel breaks the silence. "Thank you, Ryan. Anything else to report? No? Okay, let's move on to our next agenda item—growth opportunities for our leadership team."

As the others begin sharing their development goals, I spiral inward. I've researched these people. Mark won an Excellence in Quality Innovation Award. Kristen runs a Lean Manufacturing online forum. Annie's a certified Six Sigma supply chain expert. They definitely belong to this club.

Do I?

I stay quiet for the rest of the meeting. What could I possibly add?

As the staff meeting wraps up and the other managers file out of the room, Rachel calls me over.

"How are you finding your first day?" she asks.

I try to appear confident. "It's going well," I say, but Rachel sees right through me. She studies me for a moment. "What do you think of our staff team?"

I hesitate, then decide to be honest. "They're impressive. Their credentials, their experience... they're clearly well-qualified for their roles."

Rachel nods slowly. "Just as you are for yours."

I blink. Did she really believe that? Because I'm not sure I do.

"I noticed your energy shifted about halfway through the meeting," she says kindly. "Is everything okay?"

My mind scrambles for a response. I don't want her to think she made a mistake hiring me. I don't want to admit I'm already doubting myself.

She pauses for a moment before continuing. "You seem different today compared to how you were during the interview process. I want you to know that every career change comes with significant adjustments—I've experienced this myself. We hired you because of your strong technical skills and your ability to connect with people. We believed you were the right person to help your team grow, and I still hold that belief.

Her words land gently, yet they awaken something inside me. I want to believe them; I truly do.

"I'd like to share a few ideas that I believe will help you settle into this new role," she adds. "But I need to visit the factory floor right now. How about we talk more tomorrow morning at 9?"

———

My mind is spinning during my drive home that evening. I see the sun setting in my rearview mirror as I replay the day—my team's guarded expressions, the awkward silence in the staff meeting, and the way I stumbled through moments that should have felt like leadership. I'm not sure my team is excited to have me, and I'm not sure I belong among my peers. Rachel has already noticed that I'm struggling, but at least she's offering to help. That gives me something to hold onto.

As I pull into the driveway, I notice my wife's car. Emily is already home from her job as a biology professor at our state university. Just knowing she's inside with our baby daughter, Addison, brings me a sense of relief. This is exactly what I need right now.

Emily greets me with a warm smile. "How was your first day as a manager?"

I sigh, my shoulders sagging. "It wasn't what I expected, that's for sure."

"Tough day, huh?" she says gently. "Let's make that new Thai chicken salad recipe and talk about it over dinner."

That sounds perfect.

Cooking with Emily helps me shake off the weight of the day. Just like lunch with McKay, this feels natural and real. I'm not performing—I'm just being myself. Emily notices the shift in my mood. While we try to feed Addison applesauce, I tell her everything. She listens patiently and with curiosity.

"Is this what leadership is supposed to feel like?" I ask. "Is it normal to feel this unsure?"

She nods thoughtfully. "You've always been a great communicator, and your coworkers appreciate working with you. However, what you're describing seems like you're trying to lead as if you are someone else."

She's right. I don't feel like myself in this role—not yet. I've seen leadership modeled in a certain way, but perhaps that approach doesn't suit me.

———

As I go to bed that evening, a flicker of hope stirs within me. I can't shake the thought that my conversation with Rachel tomorrow might reveal new possibilities, illuminating a path forward that I hadn't imagined yet. I find myself drifting off to sleep with a sense of anticipation for what tomorrow may bring.

Chapter 2: The Awakening

The next morning, Rachel waves me into her office for our 9:00 a.m. meeting. Her space is filled with natural light and warm personal touches—photos, a small plant, and a framed quote on the wall. It feels welcoming, grounded. She's just finishing up a video call with another FutureGen manager.

"Thank you, Jared, for helping me understand your proposed approach to joint manufacturing reviews," she says, smiling into the screen. "I love new ideas, and I think yours will really benefit our division."

As she ends the call, Rachel turns to me with a warm, reassuring expression. "Tell me a little more about how yesterday went for you?" she asks, leaning back in her chair.

I offer a cautious, noncommittal response, but I can feel the urgency of her question. She nods, then shifts gears. Your new position presents opportunities for growth. I am curious, what do you consider your next developmental step that this role can provide?

My thoughts scramble as I search for something insightful to say, but the pressure is on. Before I can answer, Rachel lightens the question a bit, "I see every role—new or ongoing—as a growth opportunity. I expect you'll grow in this one too. I am interested in what you think is one area you could improve?"

I exhale, surprised by the tension I'd been carrying. It feels safe to be honest here, "I have to say, Rachel, I really admire your staff," I begin, trying to keep the tone positive. "They seem like such natural leaders. I hope I can grow into that."

Rachel nods. "They are effective leaders, Ryan—but not all of it came naturally to them. Their first days in these roles were probably not so different from yours."

I smile back, a little sheepishly. "So… you could tell I felt out of place yesterday?"

"If you hadn't, I'd be worried," she says with a chuckle. "Honestly, I'm glad you felt that way. I've been there. When I began my leadership journey, I spent a great deal of energy trying to manage how I appeared to others. Eventually, I realized I needed to shift that energy toward simply being my best self."

She pauses, then asks, "Do you remember how you felt during your interview for this role?"

I think back, the memory is clear and recent. "Honestly? Though extremely interested in this opportunity, I wasn't that nervous. I already had a secure job as an engineer, so there wasn't a great deal of pressure. I was just… being myself."

Rachel straightened up in her chair, her expression shifting to one of focus. "Can you repeat that?"

"I was just being myself during the interview."

She nods, "Exactly. That's what stood out. You were technically qualified, yes—but what got you the job was how naturally you connected with the interview team. Do you feel like that same person showed up yesterday?"

I shake my head, the truth hitting hard. "No. Not really."

"Most of us don't," she says, her tone serious now. "We may get caught up in how we're perceived. We may compare ourselves to others. It's like being back in high school, trying to fit in."

She lets that settle for a moment, then continues, "There are a few common patterns I see in new and existing leaders. One is impostor syndrome—that voice in your head asking, Do I really deserve to be here? Another is being overly comparative—measuring yourself against others based on title, age, education, or even how confident they seem. And then there's the scarcity mindset—the belief that if someone else succeeds, it somehow means you're falling behind."

She looks at me thoughtfully and asks, "Have you ever found yourself experiencing these feelings?"

I nod slowly, feeling the weight of those thoughts. "Yes, I have experienced all of those."

Rachel nods gently. "You're not alone. These patterns are common, but they can hinder our progress. They keep us focused inward, second-guessing ourselves, instead of showing up fully for others. Any of these situations can feel threatening, especially when we're stepping into something new. Often, we learn these behaviors, like self-comparison or self-doubt, from our upbringing or past work environments. But when we carry them forward in our lives, they limit our ability to be our best selves. We become too self-focused, caught in a loop of internal criticism and harsh comparisons, rather than being present and open with the people around us."

Rachel leans forward slightly, urgency in her voice. "Let me ask you something, Ryan. Think about the leaders you've worked under—the ones you and others seemed to thrive with. What were they like?"

I pause, considering the pressure to reflect weighing on me. "One person that comes to mind is Natalie—our VP. She's someone I've always respected."

Rachel nods. "I agree. How would you describe her leadership style?"

I think for a moment. "She's approachable. She genuinely takes an interest in people. I always felt like she was the real deal—someone I could trust."

Rachel then observes, "Those are powerful qualities. How about other leaders you've admired? What were they like?"

As I reflect on this, I share with her that, despite their differing leadership styles, they all had a few things in common: they inspired others while demonstrating a strong respect for them. They made people feel seen and valued—qualities that I strive to embody. Additionally, they helped individuals recognize a greater potential within themselves.

Rachel watches me process. "So, did any of those leaders seem weighed down by impostor syndrome? Did they constantly compare themselves to others or behave with a scarcity mindset?"

I jot down these terms and take a moment to reflect on them:

- *Impostor Syndrome*—These leaders seemed comfortable in their positions, not in an arrogant way, but in a friendly and confident way.

- *Overly Comparative*—They didn't need to remind you of how important they were. They treated others with dignity, regardless of their title, education, or social status.

- *Scarcity Mindset*—These leaders didn't seem threatened at all by pointing out the successes of others, which made them more approachable and relatable. They are also comfortable surrounding themselves with smart people on their team.

I tell Rachel that the great leaders I remembered did not exhibit these behaviors.

Rachel then shares, "We all feel this way sometimes. But the leaders you just described—they've learned how to resolve those feelings in positive ways, right when those doubts hit. This helps them create and maintain an environment for others to thrive around them.

"I've encountered that voice in my head questioning my worth. It can occupy a significant amount of mental space."

After a brief pause, she continues, "I remember my first management role. I walked into my director's staff meeting—just like you did yesterday—and felt completely out of place. Everyone seemed more experienced, more confident. I wasn't sure I belonged. So, to protect myself, I started copying the behavior of the other managers."

She gives a small, reflective glance. "Guess what happened? People could tell I wasn't being genuine. They had trouble trusting me. That impostor syndrome I was feeling? It turned me into an impostor of myself. I wasn't showing up fully. I was trying to wear someone else's shoes instead of my own."

Rachel's openness inspires me to keep asking, "What did you do when you realized you weren't presenting your full self? You don't seem that way now."

She looks with a sense of gratitude. "It started with a question I had to ask myself: Why am I behaving this way? Some of the answers came to me in the most unexpected place—scrolling through social media."

I raise an eyebrow, intrigued.

"I'd see these polished posts—friends and colleagues looking happy, successful, like they had it all figured out. And I'd compare myself to them. But then it hit me—those were just snapshots. They didn't show the hard moments, the messy days, the doubts. Just the highlight reel."

She pauses, then adds, "And I realized I was doing the same thing. Not just online, but at work. I wasn't showing my whole self. I was acting out a script I'd written in my head—one that was all about how I wanted to be seen. But I'm not a great actor, and that script was keeping me from being real."

Her vulnerability is captivating; she's not just talking about leadership—she's living it right here in front of me, at this very moment.

"I can relate," I say quietly, feeling the weight of my own experience. "That's exactly how I felt yesterday. Like I was trying to play a part."

Rachel nods, understanding my immediate struggle. "That's why I want to talk to you about something that changed everything for me—humility."

Humility? Where is this leading? My curiosity is piqued, so I respond, "To me, humility means staying in the background, having low self-esteem, and avoiding arrogance. Ah, I see where you're going with this. By the end of yesterday, I was feeling quite humble."

"Yes and no," Rachel interjects.

Huh? What did she mean by that? I wonder, my mind racing.

"You may have felt a bit deflated by the end of the day, which is understandable, but your definition of humility is a little incomplete. It is a much stronger and more positive trait than you think," Rachel elaborates.

"How does the word 'humility' relate to a strength?" I ask, feeling a flicker of wonder. "Wouldn't my team or your staff think less of me if I were even more 'humble' yesterday?"

"Maybe so, with your definition of humility," Rachel responds. "Let me share a more comprehensive definition of this trait, one that you will appreciate:

"Looking back at the Latin roots of the word humility:

Humilis means 'on the ground'

Humus means 'earth'

"When I think of humility, I envision being grounded—having your feet firmly planted. Being self-aware, authentic, and steady— leading from a place of clarity and internalized core values. It isn't about pretending to be more than you are or less than you are; it's about not placing yourself above or below others."

She looks at me with quiet intensity. "Tell me, Ryan—did you feel grounded yesterday? Did you feel like you were being your authentic self?"

I shake my head, the honesty of my feelings surfacing. "No. I felt like I was sinking. And I definitely wasn't being myself. Like you said earlier… I wasn't wearing my own shoes."

Rachel nods, her expression firm. "Exactly. And that's the difference. What you experienced wasn't humility—it was uncertainty. But real humility? It enables us to fully embrace our true selves and enjoy being who we are. It helps us connect, stay present, and lead with kind confidence, not control.

"Ryan, I appreciate your honesty in this discussion." Rachel's tone was steady but encouraging. "That kind of transparency is essential on my leadership team. I want you to succeed—not just in this role, but as the kind of leader people want to follow. And I believe you have the foundation to do that."

She pauses for a moment, then adds, "Humility is a key part of that foundation. But not the kind you described earlier. I call it Core Humility—because it has to be internalized first, at your core, before you can lead others with it."

I nod, intrigued. "So how do I learn to lead with that kind of humility?"

"I'd be happy to guide you through it," she replies. "It will take several conversations and time to apply, but I believe you'll find it valuable, not just for your team, but for your own growth as well. It would be great to get started as soon as you're available."

"I really appreciate that," I respond, feeling a keen sense of interest. "I'd like to begin as soon as possible."

Rachel checks her calendar. "I have time on Thursday from 11:00 to noon. We can have our initial discussion then. Does that work for you?"

"Perfect. I'll be ready."

"Great. And later, I'll also have you meet with a few of my staff who have also adopted this approach. I think you'll enjoy hearing their perspectives. In the meantime…" she jokes, "remember to wear your own shoes."

We both laugh, and I leave her office feeling lighter, like I've taken a step toward something more tangible and real. It's essential to get moving on this.

Back at my desk, I jot down a few notes to remember what we discussed:

- Humility means being grounded.
  - Having my feet firmly planted. Being self-aware, authentic, and steady—leading from a place of clarity and internalized core values.
  - It's not inflating nor diminishing who I am.
  - It's not placing myself above or below others.
  - It's about wearing my own shoes.

For the first time since taking on this role, clarity begins to take root, not just in what I need to accomplish, but in who I need to become. As I reflect on this newfound clarity, I can't help but wonder what challenges and revelations await me in the next chapter of this journey. The path ahead is gaining clarity, and I sense it will be transformative.

Chapter 3: The Mentor

My meeting with Rachel leaves me with much to ponder, especially about embracing humility and "wearing my own shoes." There's an undeniable depth to her wisdom that makes me curious to uncover more in future conversations. As I settle into my office, I reflect on whose shoes I've been metaphorically wearing this week. Stepping into a leadership role feels both exhilarating and daunting. Trying to mimic the styles of others hasn't resonated with me. So, I find myself asking: What is my leadership approach, and how can I embody humility as Rachel described?

This question evokes a vivid memory from my previous role. I recall visiting colleagues in their cubicles to connect with them. Those casual encounters enabled us to form meaningful bonds, which in turn led to improved collaboration in our work. As I begin to explore what my natural leadership approach is, I think it would be beneficial to engage my new team in a similar fashion. This feels much more authentic—these are truly the shoes I'm comfortable wearing.

I glance at my calendar and realize I have a couple of hours before the team starts packing up for the day—time to act. I spot Sean at his cubicle, deep in his work, and take a deep breath before heading over.

"Hey Sean, how's everything going?" I ask, trying to sound casual, though I can feel a tinge of nervousness in my voice.

He looks up, surprised to see me.

I continue, "Annie mentioned that you and the team did an exceptional job negotiating the OptiChain software contract. She said you ensured it reflected the interests of all key stakeholders. Her team is buzzing with anticipation."

"Hey, thanks, that's awesome to hear, Ryan," Sean replies, a genuine smile spreading across his face.

"It sounds like, in Annie's opinion, the contract is ready to go," I say, keeping the conversation light. "If you agree it's ready for signature, there's no need for me to do another review—but I'd love to hear the highlights from you."

"Absolutely!" Sean responds, visibly relieved. "I'll book some time tomorrow so we can catch up."

"Great. I'm looking forward to it," I reply, feeling the spark of connection between us. My eyes spot a golf putter in the corner of his cubicle. "So, you play golf? I've been thinking about taking lessons."

At that, Sean lights up as he dives into a spirited recount of how he and his wife took up golf a few years back, complete with the thrill of a recent hole-in-one. He mentions the office carpet is perfect for Friday putting derbies with a few team members, and extends an invitation for me to join in. I eagerly accept, sensing a bit of camaraderie.

As we wrap up our conversation, a sense of momentum builds within me. It's refreshing to connect with Sean on a more personal level. I look forward not only to our meeting tomorrow but also joining his putting derby later this week. With a burst of motivation, I decide to spend the rest of the afternoon embracing this element of my leadership approach—staying grounded and fostering connections with my team, just like I did in my previous role.

———

A few days later, Rachel and I meet again, and there's a tangible sense of anticipation in the air.

"So, how have things been since we last met?" she asks, her face keen with interest.

"I have to admit, I feel much better," I say, a sense of relief washing over me. "I've been reflecting on being more myself. In my last job, I spent part of my day connecting with people. Perhaps it was partly social, but when challenges arose, those relationships helped us support one another. That's how I naturally enjoy working—and I think it makes sense to keep doing that here."

"That's great to hear," Rachel responds enthusiastically. "You demonstrated that quality during your interview, and I'm pleased to see it resurfacing. The ability to connect and be present with others is directly related to what I want to discuss next—another layer of Core Humility."

Although Rachel's advice earlier this week eased some of my worries, I still feel somewhat inadequate around my team. While connecting with them is enjoyable, it also makes me feel more like a peer than a leader. I'm interested in what else she has to share.

"I'm all ears," I say, eager to delve deeper into this conversation.

Rachel continues, "I want to share a quote I find meaningful. It's from Melody Wilding, an executive coach at Hunter College in New York City:

"Research proves humble leadership works. Not only are self-aware leaders more effective, but they also impact the bottom line. Companies with self-aware leaders tend to have stronger financial performance. High trust also translates into better engagement."[1]

"I believe that honest self-awareness is essential to becoming a humble leader. To illustrate this point right now, I'd like to begin with an analogy," Rachel explains, as she draws a cellphone screen on her office whiteboard. "I'm sure you've taken selfies with your phone before?"

"Yes, of course," I reply, curious where this is going.

"Now, imagine downloading an app on your phone that enhances selfies," Rachel continues, sketching the outline of a person on the phone screen.

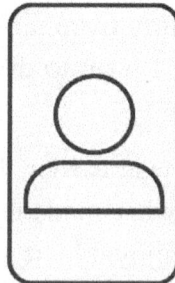

"When you take a figurative selfie with this new app, it shows your strengths and challenges—plus signs for strengths, minus signs for challenges."

She adds plus and minus symbols to the selfie.

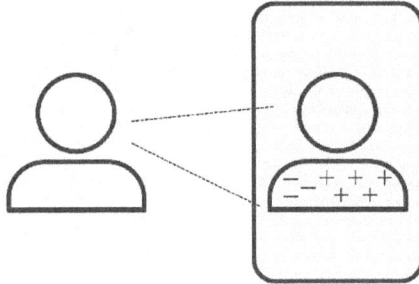

"For this analogy, challenges include weaknesses, shortcomings, or growth areas. Honestly, I probably wouldn't post this image on social media," she jokes. "But if you saw this figurative selfie right now, what would you focus on? Would you acknowledge your whole self—or just one part?"

She circles the minus signs. "Some people focus only on their challenges, ignoring their strengths.

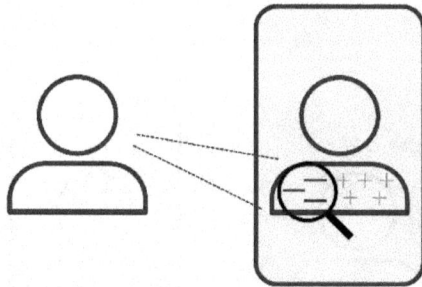

"Others feel insecure about their challenges and try to hide them, pretending they only have strengths."

She enlarges the plus signs and alters the minus signs.

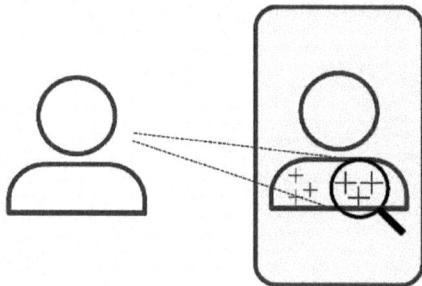

"As a leader, how do you think either of these extremes affects our ability to lead?"

I pause. "Neither fits the definition of humility you shared last time. It's like trying to be more or less than you are. Neither feels real or sustainable."

"Exactly," Rachel says. "In both cases:

- Seeing ourselves solely through the lens of our challenges or seeing ourselves as less than we truly are may seem like humility, but it actually contradicts it.
- Pretending we don't have challenges also contradicts humility, because it's not our full truth.

"In both examples, we aren't recognizing or being our whole selves. Additionally, both scenarios may be caused by or lead to:

- Feeling inferior when we compare ourselves to others.
- Wasting mental energy worrying about how we appear."

I think back on my week. Was I really comparing myself to Rachel's staff? Was I genuinely worried about how I came across to my team? I recognize that those thoughts were pulling me away from being my true self.

Rachel gestures to the drawing, "So, what do you think a humble person sees when they look at this app?"

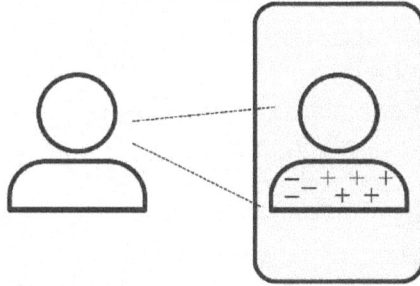

As clarity comes to mind, I say, "They see their whole selves. They recognize both their strengths and challenges simultaneously."

"That's right," she replies with a supportive expression. "They're comfortable seeing the full picture. Doing so may require applying empathy toward ourselves when reflecting on some of our challenges. So, how does this relate to our definition of humility?"

"I see that it connects with the idea of not being more or less than we truly are," I answer, feeling the weight of the moment.

Rachel agrees, then states, "Let me share another quote I came across the other day from author Parker J. Palmer. It really resonated with me…"

"*I now know myself to be a person of weakness and strength, liability and giftedness, darkness and light. I now know that to be whole means to reject none of it but to embrace all of it.*" [2]

"When we see ourselves clearly—owning our whole selves—it's easier to be authentic. We're not wasting energy hiding parts of who we are. We aren't trying to hide behind a mask we've created for ourselves."

"A mask?" I ask, curious.

"Yes," she responds, her tone urgent. "We often wear figurative masks to fit in. Let me give you an example. Early in my career, I was involved in a group technical review, and though I had questions, I didn't ask them. I was afraid it would expose to others that I lacked knowledge in that area. So, I only commented on topics I felt confident about.

"I was wearing a 'Perfectionist Mask.' I wanted to appear flawless. But that wasn't authentic, and it drained my energy. It limited my growth and likely impacted how others connected with me.

"Being your authentic self lets you offer your strengths more fully. If I'd asked those questions, I could've learned and contributed so much more. It's easier to drop the mask, be yourself, and truly engage with those around you.

"I believe we have all worn different masks throughout our lives," Rachel emphasizes. "Consider some of the other masks we may have created for ourselves:

- *Conformity Mask—Tries to blend in, avoids sharing unique ideas.*

- *Credentials Mask—Overcompensates for fear that performance won't speak for itself.*

- *Copycat Mask—Replicating the style or behavior of someone we admire, feeling less value in being ourselves."*

I reflect. I've definitely worn the Credentials Mask—trying to establish myself as a leader. And the Copycat Mask—replicating my previous manager's style. Both took up mental energy. "Yes," I say in response, "Those masks hid my true self. They kept me from showing up fully."

Rachel nods. "Humble leadership requires clear self-awareness and comfort with who we are. We urgently need to remove the masks that block our clarity. So, Ryan, when you were connecting with your team this week, were you wearing a mask?"

"No," I say, feeling a wave of relief. "I didn't need one. I was just being myself. Earlier in the week, maybe. But not then."

I lean in, eager to understand, "Rachel, how do you keep from putting on your former masks again? How do you lead in a more natural, less scripted way?"

Rachel replies, her voice steady, "I have learned that there are three initial steps that can help us become more self-aware now. These steps help create an environment that enables us to internalize humility at our core. I promise, they've helped me feel more confident in embracing my whole self and appreciating humility more deeply." Rachel then writes down the three steps:

- Recognizing our Value and Potential
- Appreciating our Uniqueness
- Having Gratitude and Grace

"Once we're more self-aware, we're better equipped to lead with humility toward others. However, before we go there, I'd like you to speak with a few members of my team who have recently gone through this process. They've found it invaluable—and I believe you will too. Interested?"

"Absolutely," I say, feeling a sense of urgency. "Who should I meet with first?"

"Do you remember Annie, our senior manager of Production Planning and Control? I'll set up a time for you to meet soon. She will expertly guide you through the first step: Recognizing Our Value and Potential."

Back at my desk, I notice the invite pop up—Monday afternoon with Annie. Perfect. I'll need that time to reflect on everything Rachel shared.

I open my phone and add the following notes from today:

- To see my "whole self," I need to acknowledge both my strengths and challenges simultaneously.

- Wearing a "mask" to hide my perceived shortcomings prevents others from seeing the full extent of who I am and drains my mental energy in the process.

As I reflect on my notes, I am curious how the concept of recognizing my value and potential will deepen my self-awareness. With Annie's guidance, I'm eager to uncover the insights that await.

Chapter 4: Recognizing My Value and Potential

It's finally Saturday. Emily and I are pushing Addison in her stroller toward the neighborhood pickleball court, eager to squeeze in a morning match before the day gets away from us. Little do I know, this game will reflect some essential lessons I'm grappling with about fully recognizing my strengths and challenges.

My uncle, Brian, the one who introduced us to pickleball a few months back, is already at the court, stretching beside his cooler brimming with sodas and snacks. He always thinks ahead. Moments later, McKay—my coworker and an enthusiastic cyclist—pulls up on his e-bike.

We find a shaded corner for Addison to play with her toys while we warm up. I introduce McKay to Brian, and they quickly strategize on one side of the court while Emily and I do the same. We start our game as McKay serves a perfect shot to Emily's corner. She snaps it back right at Brian's feet. He shifts too late and misses— a rare error for him. Side out.

Emily serves next. McKay returns it high to me, and I send it toward Brian, who gently taps it into the kitchen—a designated area with specific rules. I rush forward and return the ball before it bounces, but my momentum carries me into the kitchen.

"Fault! Opponent in the kitchen!" Brian announces with a sly grin, purposefully louder than necessary.

"Thanks, Brian. Now the whole neighborhood knows!" I joke back.

Brian and McKay exchange a triumphant fist bump, their faces alight with the thrill of their performance. We play three intense games, and in a nail-biting finish, Team Brian/McKay narrowly clinched the victory, winning two out of three.

"Snack break!" Brian calls, and we gather Addison to head to the picnic table where the guys are already unpacking snacks.

"That was fun—and thanks for the snacks," Emily says. "Can I grab one of those lime waters?"

"Of course," Brian replies. "You two have come a long way. I remember when Ryan used to forget to let the serve bounce before hitting it, like the rule requires."

"And remembering that you have a very capable teammate…" Emily adds with a teasing grin.

"Today, you only did that a few times. Nice improvement!" Brian acknowledges.

"I owe it all to you, Brian. Everything I've learned about pickleball comes from your coaching," I say earnestly.

As I reflect on how far I've come in this game, I think back to Rachel's phone app analogy—how strengths and challenges can be seen as pluses and minuses. My pickleball skills have shifted from a minus to a plus. "This reminds me of a conversation I had with my new director, Rachel," I say, as I share the high-level points of her analogy with them.

"I heard her share these concepts during a brown bag session," McKay replies. "It helped me rethink self-awareness and humility. It made me reflect on how I show up around others."

"So, how are you applying this in your new role?" Brian asks, genuinely curious.

"Rachel is involving a few of her staff members to share steps toward becoming a humble leader. What I'm learning is already inspiring me to make changes in how I present myself to my team. I'm leaning into my natural strengths instead of trying to imitate others. For example, connecting with people is something that comes naturally to me. I can see how behaving in this way helps build trust within my team. I can also see the value of recognizing my challenges and seeing my whole self."

"Like recognizing your tendency to forget to let the serve bounce before hitting it," quips McKay with a smile.

"Exactly," I respond. Having the confidence to see my whole self enables me to recognize and address my challenges, even in pickleball, more easily. Depending on the challenge, I may also choose to focus on transforming it into a strength.

"There's so much more to learn on this topic. I'm looking forward to meeting with one of Rachel's staff members, Annie, on Monday to discuss it further."

"Thanks for sharing that," Brian says. "I never thought of humility as a strength. I always thought it meant being timid or less noticeable. Let's play again next Saturday. I'll refill the cooler, and we can talk more about this topic after Team Brian/McKay's next win."

"And we'll teach you more about humility during our decisive victory," McKay adds with a playful nudge.

Emily rolls her eyes, jokingly amused. "Oh, I get it… Challenge accepted!"

—

Monday morning arrives, and I'm eager to delve deeper into the lessons on humility. I make my way to Annie's office for our meeting, with anticipation coursing through me.

"Come on in!" she calls when I knock. "Rachel mentioned you had a great conversation last week. She asked me to share one of the key takeaways I had from a similar discussion we had a year ago."

"It's reassuring to know I'm not the only one she's talked to about humility," I say with a smile. "At first, I thought I was a unique case."

Annie smiles back. "Rachel shared her thoughts on Core Humility with many of us. It helps me lead more authentically by bringing my true self into my leadership style. I've been looking forward to our meeting."

"Where do we start?" I ask, excitement evident.

Annie emphasizes that the first crucial step to becoming a more self-aware leader is recognizing our value and potential. "How can we be authentic if we don't know who we are?" she asks seriously.

Annie's expression shifts abruptly as a cherished memory rises to the surface. "This reminds me of an experience I had during my industrial engineering program in college," she begins. "We were given the incredible opportunity to embark on a semester-long class focused on a real-world project—a water initiative in a rural village in Africa. The moment I heard about it, I felt an undeniable pull. It was a chance to truly make a difference, though I had no idea just how profoundly it would shape my life.

Her tone grows more animated as she dives deeper into the experience. "From the outset, I realized this wasn't going to be a typical class project. The stakes were high, and people were depending on us. I had to rise to the occasion—not just as a student, but as a key contributor to the team. I found myself relying on all my resources: the technical knowledge gained from my courses, the organizational skills developed from part-time jobs, and the communication abilities fostered through group projects and internships."

She beams, almost lost in the memory. "It was challenging. There were setbacks, language barriers, and countless moments of self-doubt. But we powered through. And when we finally got that system up and running—when we saw families filling their containers with clean water for the first time—it was an overwhelming moment. It wasn't just about our achievement; it was also about the profound discovery of who I really am.

Annie's tone transitions to the present. "That experience taught me I'm capable of more than I ever thought possible. I uncovered strengths I didn't even know I possessed, and I learned that challenges aren't mere obstacles; they're invitations for growth. That project didn't just transform the village—it transformed me.

"Speaking of transformation, I want to chat about self-awareness. Let's quickly look up the definition of this word. Indeed.com defines it as:

Self-Awareness - A mindful consciousness of your strengths, weaknesses, actions, and presence.[3]

"Thinking about the topic of recognizing our value and potential, everything we are today is the result of what we've learned, applied, and experienced up to this point. All that we will become in the future will be built upon this foundation. Did Rachel share her famous 'phone app' analogy with you?"

I confirmed that she did. Annie then drew this image on her iPad for discussion, circling the '+' signs.

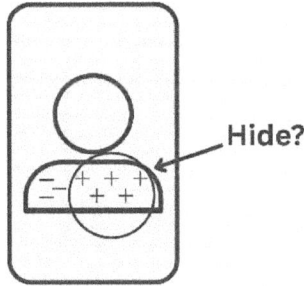

"Ryan, do you think humility means hiding or not fully utilizing our full value and potential?" Annie asked, her curiosity evident.

I pause to consider her question. Are we showing off when we make full use of our skills? Perhaps sometimes, but if humility is about being authentic, we shouldn't feel compelled to hide our abilities.

"I think we shouldn't hide our strengths—as long as we are not using them in a boastful way," I responded thoughtfully.

"Exactly," Annie said, nodding in agreement. "Using them just to show off isn't humility. But fully using them authentically—with our feet on the ground—is." I recall a quote from Patrick Lencioni, author of The Ideal Team Player, which resonates with this idea:"

"Truly humble people do not see themselves as greater than they are, but neither do they discount their talents and contributions." [4]

She revises the drawing. "What about our challenges? Should we broadcast them to others?"

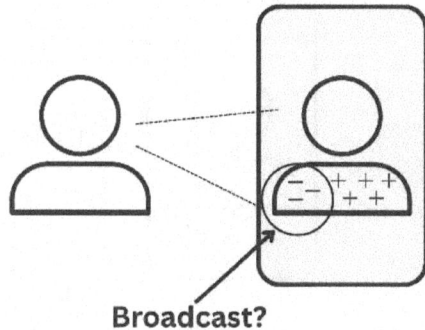

Broadcast?

That's harder. "I don't see the benefit of letting everyone know about all of my challenges. That would lead to an awkward conversation," I say. "However, once I trust someone, I would feel comfortable sharing a few."

"I agree," she says, her face intent. "It's healthy to acknowledge our challenges. We don't need to be embarrassed by the fact that we have them since we all have them. If we can reach this level of self-awareness, we will gain better visibility and acceptance of ourselves. When we feel safe showing up this way around others, it can create a great bond of trust with them."

Annie then poses an interesting question: "Do you think there's value in our challenges?"

I consider this question. I've always seen challenges more as burdens, a weight that drags me down, rather than anything truly valuable.

"Perhaps they help keep me humble in the right way?" I suggest, hoping this contributes to the conversation.

"Yes, when we reflect on our challenges in a constructive manner, they can help us remain grounded and protect us from arrogance," Annie says. "Furthermore, I believe there are times when these challenges can add value. They can shape our identity and enhance our authenticity.

"Take Abraham Lincoln, for example—the 16th president of the United States. I recently read a biography about him, and it was clear he faced significant challenges. But what really struck me was how those hardships helped shape his character."

She lists them out emphatically: "Little formal education. The loss of his mother at an early age. Multiple business failures. A string of political defeats. And a lifelong struggle with depression.

"And yet," she prompts me, "how do you think those experiences shaped Lincoln's character?"

"Well," I reply, thinking quickly, "from what I've read, he seemed incredibly reasonable and empathetic. He didn't act like he was above others, even as a president."

Annie nods, confirming my response. "Exactly. He was grounded. His challenges didn't diminish him—they deepened him. They made him more approachable, more genuine."

She adds, "I also learned that Lincoln was teased in school. To cope, he turned to humor and storytelling. That skill helped him later in life—he became a powerful communicator. His stories helped him connect, persuade, and put people at ease."

"From what you are saying, it seems that being honest about our challenges can open the door to growth," I realize. "Some challenges can definitely knock us down—but others can help shape us into who we are meant to become."

Annie then shares a compelling quote from author Daniel Friedland:

"There is no need to deny parts of who you are; every part of yourself is important and serves as a teaching tool." [5]

"Looking back on my life, I have to agree with that," I say. "Public speaking was a real challenge for me as a kid."

"You're not alone there," Annie replies. "Most people struggle with it."

"I remember taking speech classes in school and feeling so nervous," I continue. "I would always wait until the very last moment to volunteer to share my speech. I'd sit there, dreading my turn and feeling sick the whole time."

Annie then queries, "So how did that change for you?"

"One day, I just asked myself—why am I putting myself through this? Whether I go first or last, I still have to give the same speech. The only difference is how long I feel miserable beforehand. So, the next time our class gave speeches, I raised my hand first. And you know what? It worked. My speech was over before the nerves could take over, and I actually enjoyed listening to my classmates afterward."

I pause for a moment, then add, "Over time, I realized that I had more energy and clarity when I was one of the early speakers in that class. It helped me not just to read words, but to communicate and teach ideas."

"Wow, thanks for sharing that, Ryan," Annie says. "Whether that was a challenge or a weakness—or both—it's a great example of choosing growth. You moved through your fear and turned it into a strength. I'm sure the nervousness you felt while waiting your turn shaped your experience, and your decision to change helped you become a better speaker. Do you think that confidence carried into other parts of your life?"

"Come to think of it, yes," I say, the memory still fresh. "I tried out for the football team shortly afterward. That experience in speech class gave me the confidence to take on something that normally felt pretty intimidating."

Annie nods, her thoughts clearly aligning. "So, I think we've both learned that some of our challenges are there for a reason—and they can have real value. Acknowledging them and recognizing how they've shaped us is essential. When we combine that with a full awareness of our strengths, we start to see ourselves more clearly."

She continues, "And that's where humility comes in. When we're self-aware, we realize we don't know everything—and that there's always more to learn from our experiences and others. That mindset helps us stay teachable and open to feedback. It's freeing to know we don't have to pretend to have all the answers. We can lead with a healthy curiosity and a willingness to grow."

"Thanks for connecting those dots for me, Annie," I say, genuinely appreciative. "I really like that phrase—'healthy curiosity.' Life feels so much more enjoyable when we're eager to learn from others."

"You're very welcome, Ryan," Annie says warmly. "I've enjoyed our conversation, and I know Rachel will have even more to share with you about humility. What she taught me helped me lead more authentically—and made my experience as a manager so much more fulfilling. I think you'll really enjoy what's next."

I thank Annie for her time and quickly add the following notes to my phone, feeling a sense of urgency to capture every insight before they slip away.

- Humility includes utilizing all of my strengths—they're part of my authentic self.

- Challenges have value. I don't need to broadcast or feel embarrassed by them. Instead, I can see them as future opportunities and tools for growth.

- A clear self-awareness enables me to cultivate humility and helps me remain teachable.

Reflecting on our conversation helps me consider how I can better embrace my true self. I feel a spark of excitement about the possibilities ahead. What other lessons might I discover on this journey of growth?

Chapter 5: Embracing My Unique Approach

As I drive home that evening, I reflect on Annie's insights, especially her final thought about how embracing and being her authentic self has significantly transformed her management experience. Her genuine love for leading her team contrasts sharply with how I felt during my first few days on the job. What she shared resonates deeply with me, making me realize that fully embracing who I am is not only more effective but also far more enjoyable. Trying to be someone I'm not is nothing short of stressful and unnecessary. As I pull into the driveway, I notice that I'm in a much better state of mind than I was just a week ago. I genuinely feel like I'm on a more positive path, and I'm eager to continue exploring this topic.

—

The next morning at the office, Rachel stops by my desk, keenly curious about my conversation with Annie.

"It went great!" I say enthusiastically, feeling a surge of energy. "Annie is an excellent coach and leader," I continue. "She gave me a fresh perspective on recognizing my value and potential. Learning that humility allows me to fully utilize my strengths and view my challenges as opportunities for growth was liberating. It's helping me see the value of being more authentic—and I know it will help me connect even better with my team."

"I love it!" Rachel replies, her excitement evident. "A clear awareness of your strengths and challenges is a vital first step toward being a humble leader. They all have value and represent your authentic self. Additionally, feeling comfortable embracing your own unique approach as you share that value is another aspect of self-awareness. Are you ready to learn more about this?"

Naturally, I quickly agreed. Rachel smiles and asks, "Do you remember Kristen from our staff meeting? She's the senior manager of our Process Improvement and Optimization team. I'd like you to meet with her to discuss this topic of embracing your unique approach. I'll set it up right away."

I thanked Rachel, and soon after, I'm pleasantly surprised by an invite from Kristen for 1:00 p.m. that afternoon. That was quick.

During lunch, McKay and I reconnect. He animatedly recounts the "glorious victory" he and Brian celebrated last weekend on the pickleball court, complete with dramatic play-by-plays. I laugh and remind him of the fact that I was there. Then, I share some interesting insights that Annie gave me that morning. I mix these ideas into our conversation, making the lunch feel more like a casual brainstorming session. The conversation flows effortlessly, blending humor with meaningful insights. It becomes a memorable moment in the day. Before we know it, our lunch hour turns into a nice highlight of the day.

After lunch, I head to Kristen's office, curious about what will come next. She's just finishing up her lunch and greets me warmly.

Her office is organized and inviting, decorated with family photos and a race medal hanging beside her computer.

"Thanks for meeting with me," I say, genuinely appreciative. "Rachel's been teaching me a lot about humble leadership."

Kristen smiles knowingly. "Yes—Core Humility. It's one of Rachel's favorite topics. She had me meet with her staff when I joined her group a few years ago. I'm glad she's continuing the tradition. She asked me to talk with you about something I really appreciate: embracing our unique approach. But before we dive in, I'd love to hear more about you."

I open up about my background, touching on my family and my newfound passion for pickleball, a sport that's quickly captured my enthusiasm. In turn, Kristen shares her captivating journey, revealing the twists and turns that have shaped her experiences.

"As you can see from the photos, my husband and I are raising three boys—Henry, Ethan, and Jack. They call themselves the 'Three Musketeers,' and they definitely live up to the name. I've been with FutureGen for ten years and have led the Process Improvement and Optimization team for the past two."

I point to the medal on her wall, curiosity piquing. "What's the story behind that?"

Kristen laughs lightly. "That medal? It's actually a reminder for me to stay humble."

"Humble? You'll have to explain that one," I reply, genuinely intrigued.

"I'd love to," she says earnestly. "It ties directly into our topic of embracing our unique approach. A few years ago, I signed up for my first half marathon and followed a 12-week training plan. I wasn't worried about speed; I just wanted to complete the race. About six weeks in, I went for a morning run along the lake near my home. I noticed a man running ahead of me, and guess what? I started gaining on him. Although I mentioned that I wasn't focused on speed, I'll admit—I felt a little proud to be catching up with him.

"As I passed him, I made a friendly comment about the weather and asked how far he was running. He replied, a bit out of breath, 'I'm on mile 18. How about you?'

"I laughed at myself as I said, 'I'm on mile one.' In that moment, I felt a wave of embarrassment. I had been comparing myself to someone who was running a completely different race than I.

"That moment stayed with me. I realized how easy it is to compare ourselves to others without knowing their full story. I had created a narrative that made me feel superior—until I learned the truth. It reminded me that we are all running our own race. Since then, I have also learned that even when we are running our own race and compare ourselves to our past selves, we should do so with kindness."

Kristen gestures toward the medal. "That's why I keep it there. It reminds me to focus on my own progress and to celebrate others without letting comparison steal my joy. I love this quote that some have attributed to 19th-century author Oscar Wilde, which encourages me to strive in my own way."

"Be yourself; everyone else is already taken."

Kristen's voice turns more serious. "This medal serves as a daily reminder to run my own race and to remember that others are doing the same. I do not need to compare my performance with that of others. Why should I let someone else's performance determine my happiness today? We all have different experiences, starting points, and natural abilities. Each of us is truly unique.

"I can run my own race while maintaining a generous attitude towards others' achievements. Nobody is exactly like me, whether as a runner, a manager, a mom, or in any other role. That's something worth celebrating! I approach these areas in my own unique way, and I believe that's pretty cool. I am the only me there is."

"So, how do you apply that mindset at work right now?" I ask. "I'll admit, I've compared myself to others, especially when it comes to things like salary increases. It feels good to know you did better than someone else—even just for a moment."

Kristen nods in agreement, "That's natural. It's great to be rewarded for your performance. However, when we focus on comparing ourselves to others, we risk losing a fundamental aspect of humility: staying grounded and not placing ourselves above or below anyone else. It's essential to celebrate your successes and learn from your shortcomings. Let others do the same in their own space.

"As Stephen R. Covey emphasizes in *The 7 Habits of Highly Effective People*, highly effective individuals focus on their circle of influence—what they can control—rather than being reactive to external comparisons. He also teaches that those with an abundance mentality can genuinely celebrate others' success without feeling diminished themselves."[6]

"Why should someone else's performance affect your self-worth or attitude today? Their achievements belong to them, not to you. What you can control is your decision to do your best using your unique strengths and approach. If someone else happens to perform better than you, that is their choice, not yours.

"Think about it. If someone is doing better than you and jealousy kicks in, how might that affect you?" Kristen asks, looking at me thoughtfully.

"I'd probably feel resentful," I admit, feeling a bit uncomfortable.

"What if, instead, you chose to be happy for that person's achievement?" she suggests. "How would that change your feelings?"

"I'd feel a lot better," I respond, realizing the truth in her words.

Kristen continued, "Who ultimately controls the outcome in either situation?"

"I do," I answer after a moment's thought.

"And how much does that other person influence your choice?" she asks, prompting deeper reflection.

"Minimal impact," I reply. "It's really up to me how I choose to react."

"So, which choice leaves you in a better place?" Kristen asks again, prompting me to reflect further.

"Of course, the positive response," I affirm.

"Correct. The key word is choice," noted Kristen, her tone earnest. "You have control over your choices and must live with the results of those choices. Others' performances result from their own choices, and no rule states that you have to allow their choices to impact you negatively. While it may feel instinctive to react negatively, why not choose to be generous towards others and celebrate their successes? This attitude helps maintain a humble confidence within us, creating a more positive environment in which to navigate our lives.

"If we are eager for growth, we can even allow the success of others to inspire us to improve in our own ways. There's no need to slow down just because someone else is excelling. I have found that when I genuinely feel happy for someone else's success, it generates greater positive mental energy for my own performance.

Conversely, engaging in unhealthy comparisons can drain our energy and hinder our progress."

"You've given me a lot to think about, Kristen," I said, feeling a shift in my perspective. "Adopting this mindset will require a bit of 'reprogramming' on my part. You're right, though. It seems to hinge on the concept of 'choice.' I can choose how to react in the situations you mentioned. I also see the value in remaining humble when I perform better than others."

"I think I understand where you're going with that thought, Ryan," Kristen replied, with an expression of interest.

"Using your same logic, when I notice that I am performing better than my coworkers, it's equally important not to let it go to my head. If I did, I would fall back into comparison mode, allowing others' performance to dictate my mood, which contradicts the importance of staying grounded.

"Relating this back to your example of running, it reminds me of one of those race videos where two runners are neck and neck— and the one who glances sideways loses focus and falls behind."

"Exactly," Kristen said, nodding. "Comparison drains mental energy and distracts us from being our authentic selves. But when we stay grounded and focus on our own race, we can better appreciate our journey."

As we wrap up our conversation, I thank Kristen for her time and insights, feeling inspired by our discussion. She shares that she also enjoyed it and looks forward to future collaborations. She also expresses her appreciation for Sarah's work on the AMI project and mentions hearing about the progress made in resolving that project's testing issue.

Back at my desk, I decided to check in with Sarah sooner rather than later to hear more about the recent testing progress Kristen mentioned.

"Hi Sarah! Do you have a few minutes to catch up?" I ask, eager to hear her updates.

"Yes, I just finished a call with our test engineer," she replies. "Thanks again for your flexibility with the testing data issue."

"Of course," I say, feeling motivated to support her efforts. "Kristen mentioned your team identified the root cause of the testing issue. When she brought it up, I realized there were other ways to address the schedule slip, beyond just working more hours. You and your team are the experts, and I want to support the approach you feel is best."

Even though I had just told Sarah she knew more than I did, I felt confident saying it. This was new for me. Leadership isn't about being the smartest person in the room—it's about enabling others to succeed.

"Thanks again for trusting us with this issue," Sarah says, her enthusiasm evident. "Our test engineer found the corrupt data source and is generating a new data set. We'll resume testing tomorrow. The team is so excited; they've set a goal to catch up by the end of next week. Is that offer for overtime still open?"

"Whatever you need," I reply, ready to support her. "Just let me know."

As we wrap up, I realize something important: trusting Sarah to lead didn't diminish my own leadership—it strengthened it and deepened our working relationship.

Back in my office, I open my phone and quickly jot down a few notes from the day, feeling the weight of these realizations.

- Each of us is running our own unique race, with individual strengths and challenges. Embracing my unique approach is both healthy and empowering.

- Comparing myself to others consumes valuable mental energy. It can prevent me from being my authentic self and distract me from self-awareness.

- I can cultivate a more productive and positive mindset by celebrating the successes of others.

- An additional lesson learned from my chat with Sarah: Confidently trusting the experts on my team doesn't take away from my leadership—it enhances it.

Today's experience was enlightening, broadening my perspective in unexpected ways. I'm eager to see how this journey continues to unfold, and I sense that more is yet to come, waiting to be revealed.

Chapter 6: Practicing Gratitude and Grace

It's game day, and Brian and McKay are already warming up on the pickleball court when Emily and I arrive, Addison tucked into her stroller. They're clearly taking this game seriously, and I feel a rush of excitement—the competition is on.

"Hold on," Emily exclaims, her eyes wide. "They're wearing matching shirts! When did this happen?"

"Hey, good morning, everyone." McKay calls out, pointing to his bright orange shirt, which boldly displays "Net Rangers" on the front and his name on the back. "Pretty cool, don't you think? Brian and I came up with this name ourselves!"

"Very classy," I reply, half-joking. "What you lack in skills, you certainly make up for in style."

"It feels like a good day for a 'challenge round!'" Brian declares, glancing up at the sky as if proclaiming this to the world.

Ah, Brian and his challenge rounds. We compete for a can of soda, a Costco hot dog, or whatever he has in his game cooler—and of course, bragging rights. Today, the prize is a can of Pringles potato chips. The stakes feel higher than ever.

We set up baby Addison in a safe, shaded corner of the court and dive into what turns out to be a fiercely competitive match. The Net Rangers snag the first game with a score of 11–8, and their confidence swells, fueled by their new shirts. But Emily and I quickly shut that down, winning game two 11–4, leaving the Net Rangers looking deflated and desperate.

"Five-minute break!" Brian shouts, and a wave of relief washes over us. We definitely could use a breather. We walk over to check on Addison, who has been quietly focused on her toys. Meanwhile, Brian and McKay pull to the side, whispering and exchanging glances that suggest a plan is forming to change their current trajectory.

The final match escalates quickly. With an 11–11 tie, we know we must win by two points, and that can of Pringles has suddenly transformed into something greater.

The score oscillates dramatically. Once again, we find ourselves tied at 15–15. Emily serves, driving the ball right down the middle—untouchable. We surge ahead by one. Then something unexpected happens as Emily announces, "This one is for the Pringles! 16–15–2!"

Noticing Brian is playing a bit back; she serves the ball just barely over the net. When Brian hears Emily announce "Pringles," he can't resist glancing at the Pringles can displayed on the side of the court. That brief distraction delays his reaction just long enough for us to clinch the decisive point—and win the match.

Brian and McKay try to contest Emily's cunning strategy, but they know it's a lost cause.

Gathering around the picnic table along with baby Addison, we feel the thrill of victory. True to tradition, Brian opens the game cooler to share its contents. Emily and I hold up our trophy—the can of Pringles—proudly thanking the Net Rangers for the worthy challenge.

After discussing the enjoyable and competitive experience of our game, Brian asks how my coaching sessions with Rachel are progressing. I mention that she's arranged for me to meet with her staff to explore new aspects of humility. I'm also scheduled to meet with Mark on Monday to discuss practicing gratitude and grace—a topic that suddenly feels increasingly important.

While enjoying the snacks from Brian's cooler, I recap my insightful meeting with Annie, who described humility as not holding back on fully utilizing our abilities, enabling us to be authentic. I compare that lesson to the competitive yet supportive essence of our pickleball match, where each of us brought our unique strengths to the game. I share Annie's thoughts that our challenges can hold value—they represent true opportunities for growth.

I share Kristen's emphasis on embracing our unique approach, explaining how comparing ourselves to others can drain vital mental energy and distract us from our authenticity.

"Those are interesting perspectives on humility," Brian says, his expression curious. "Did this influence your approach during today's 'questionable' victory?"

"Now that I think about it, it did," I reply, my mind racing with the implications. "And it made the game so much more enjoyable for me."

"Of course, because you won!" McKay chimes in, laughing.

"Haha. I admit the win was nice. But honestly, it was more about maintaining a positive mindset throughout the game. I wanted to win, yes, but seeing the Net Rangers play well was uplifting too. Just last week, Kristen emphasized that having a generous attitude toward others' successes helps us stay grounded. When you won the first game, I genuinely tried to feel happy for your win. Maybe that mindset boosted my performance in the subsequent games and made the match even more enjoyable."

"Interesting," McKay ponders. "Supporting a competitor's success feels unnatural to me, but I see how it can help you focus on your own performance. Others' success shouldn't distract from our own best efforts."

"Exactly," I respond, feeling energized. "Resisting the temptation to compare ourselves helps us make better progress on our own path."

"Hey, who wants to help us celebrate that amazing victory we just achieved?" Emily asks, eagerly popping the lid off the Pringles. "By the way, where did you get those Net Rangers shirts? Ryan and I might need matching ones also—and a team name."

McKay and Brian exchange mock looks of alarm before quickly changing the subject, their panic bringing a smile to my face as they start planning next Saturday's rematch.

—

On Monday, I arrive at Mark's office for our scheduled discussion, feeling excited about this next layer of leadership humility. He's the senior manager of Quality in Rachel's department and is just wrapping up a conversation with one of his team members. As he greets me, I notice a picture of his family next to a Lego spaceship displayed on the side of his desk.

"That's a pretty nice Lego model your kid made," I say, eager to break the ice. "I remember playing with those when I was young."

"Haha! You're looking at the designer and builder of this original Lego structure," Mark replies with a grin on his face.

I hadn't realized adults assembled Lego models. My face flushes red—I've just implied he's playing with children's toys. I need to recover quickly.

"Wow, you designed this?" I ask, trying to steer the conversation in a positive direction.

"Yes, and I hear you," Mark says, assisting in my recovery. "My kid loves Legos, and so do I. Honestly, I credit my interest in manufacturing to this toy. I see what we create at FutureGen as intricate Lego-like assemblies—each one built to exact specs and quality standards to deliver an excellent product."

"Sounds like you're in the perfect industry," I say, feeling the conversation flow more naturally now.

"I think so," Mark replies. "And what makes it even better is the culture Rachel has built in her department. She encourages us to find joy in our work, and part of that joy comes from bringing our best selves to the table and being open to new challenges. Rachel asked me to talk with you about an aspect of Core Humility that's close to my heart: practicing gratitude and grace toward ourselves."

"Those sound like words I'd hear in church," I say, chuckling to lighten the mood.

"I thought the same thing at first," Mark laughs, glancing at the clock. "But they're just as valuable in the business world. Hey, we're probably both hungry. I hope you like a good delicatessen. There's a place that serves an amazing green garlic sauce, which they use on their sandwiches. You've got to try it. I'll drive."

We head to Lorenzo's Deli, the anticipation building as we order sandwiches, and Mark is right—the green garlic sauce is incredible.

As we eat our sandwiches and get to know each other, I circle back to his earlier point, eager to dig deeper. "So how do you apply gratitude and grace in the business world?" I ask.

"Great question. Think back to your first day as a senior manager," Mark says. "You probably felt like most of us do—stressed, uncertain, hoping to connect with your team."

I laugh, the memory hitting close to home. "That's exactly how I felt. I guess it showed."

"Totally normal," Mark reassures me. "So what were you focused on that day?"

I told him I was trying to be like other leaders instead of being myself.

"Think about it. How productive is it to focus on being something we're not?" Mark asks, his intensity rising a notch. "That's where gratitude comes in—appreciating what we bring to the table."

"That blends into and adds another layer to what Annie and Kristen shared—recognizing our value and being comfortable with our unique approach," I say, feeling the connection deepen.

"Exactly," Mark nods, emphasizing his point. "Gratitude boosts self-awareness, which is essential for true humility. If we concentrate too much on what we lack, it can harm our mindset. What kind of state do you think that puts us in?"

"I don't feel like I can fully function when I let that happen," I admit, sensing the truth in his words. "I get stuck focusing on my shortcomings and feel flat-footed around others."

"And that prevents us from fully utilizing the tools we have. Ryan, can you share with me what you consider as one of your strengths? Please, don't be 'humble' about it," Mark jokes with a smile.

After some thought, I share, "Come to think of it, I am very detail-oriented," recalling how this strength benefited me in my previous engineering role. "In engineering, precision is crucial, and my focus on the specifics ensured that our designs were innovative while also meeting safety and performance standards."

"That is a wonderful strength, and not everyone has it. You may be so accustomed to it that you don't always recognize you possess a strength such as this. Acknowledging and appreciating your strengths enables you to use them more purposely, rather than letting your mind focus on wishing you had what others have," he explains.

He continues, leaning in slightly, "Gratitude also includes being thankful for those who helped shape us—mentors, teachers, parents, even a higher power. This mindset further strengthens us in being grounded and approachable."

As I take another bite of my sandwich, I realize how powerful that concept is. Gratitude shifts our focus from what we lack to what we have—and that changes everything. I can feel that change providing clarity within me, and it's a feeling I want to hold onto.

"Rachel also taught me about grace," Mark says. "Think back to your first day again. How did you treat yourself? Were you patient or harsh?"

"I was discouraged," I admit, feeling the weight of that memory. "When I made a mistake, I was hard on myself."

"Why?" Mark presses, clearly wanting me to dig deeper.

"I felt like I had to prove myself. And when I didn't, I felt ashamed—like maybe I wasn't cut out for the job."

"And how did that impact the rest of your day?" he asks with genuine interest.

"I felt down. I withdrew a bit in meetings."

"So, it temporarily affected your performance," Mark says empathetically. "I remember you mentioning earlier that you have a baby daughter who might start walking soon. What are your expectations for her on the first day?"

"Probably just a step or two," I say while smiling as I picture her first attempt. "She'll improve over time."

"Exactly. So why expect yourself to be running on day one of a new role?" Mark asks, his face showing insight. "We give others space to grow—but forget to give it to ourselves."

"That's true," I reflect, feeling the realization sink in. "I wanted to succeed right away, but when I didn't, it threw me off."

"Now imagine giving yourself permission to stretch, learn, even make mistakes. If you did that, how do you think your first day would have gone?"

"I probably wouldn't have spiraled. I would have stayed more engaged," I acknowledge.

"That's the power of grace," Mark emphasizes. "It's treating ourselves with kindness and patience, especially during growth. If we can feel confident with others seeing us go through our learning process while we seek a new skill or have a new assignment, we are more likely to successfully pursue new growth opportunities."

"Doesn't it feel awkward when others observe us during our learning process?" I challenge, feeling a weight of vulnerability.

"It depends on your perspective," Mark responds earnestly. "What's more important—always appearing polished while accomplishing little, or embracing growth, even if it's imperfect?"

"When I think about humility, it's clear—worrying about appearances contradicts being authentic. Being okay with others seeing our growth actually supports being humble," I say, feeling the truth resonate within me. But a lingering question remains. "Won't people still think less of us?"

"Moving beyond the perceived embarrassment of appearing to learn something new in front of others is crucial," Mark insists. "One of the wonderful aspects of extending grace to ourselves is that it fosters a more supportive internal environment, enabling us to take steps toward growth and learn from our experiences, even the negative ones. Letting go of the need to always appear our best—whether in front of others or even in our own eyes—can actually boost our confidence in embracing new challenges. For instance, I kept mispronouncing a word during a presentation last week. Instead of being embarrassed, I saw the humor in it and laughed at the situation kindly. This actually created a better connection with my audience that improved their engagement afterwards," Mark notes, his voice full of gratitude.

"This approach reminds me of people I know who are eager for personal growth," I mention, feeling inspired. "I can't imagine them being too worried about how others perceive them. They thrive on trying new things and, over time, become skilled at them. These individuals seem to possess an adventurous spirit and tend to adopt an attitude of self-encouragement during their learning experiences. They can even joke—much like you did—about the mistakes they make along the way."

"Exactly, Ryan, I have to show you a few sketches I made that reminds me of gratitude and grace," Mark says, clearly eager to share.

"Last year, my wife and I saved up for a trip to Italy, leaving our son, Matthew, with his grandparents. While visiting the Gallery of the Academy of Florence to see the statue of David, we came across the statue of Saint Matthew from Biblical times. I thought our son, Matthew, would love to know that there is a statue that shares his name. I made a rough sketch on a notepad after our visit. I became intrigued by this statue because the front half was beautifully carved, while the back half was still a roughly cut block of marble," Mark shares as he eagerly shows me a copy of this sketch.

Mark continues, "Michelangelo sculpted Saint Matthew in 1506. It was intended for a series of the twelve apostles for the Florence Cathedral but was left unfinished when Michelangelo was called to Rome to work for Pope Julius II."

"It reminds me of Han Solo frozen in the carbonite block in the *Star Wars* movie *The Empire Strikes Back*," I joke.

"Yes, that's a great way of looking at it," Mark responds with a laugh. "This sculpture reminds me of how we should treat ourselves and others. The front of the statue, which was nearly complete, represents how we have all grown to a certain extent. It symbolizes the development of our abilities, showcasing the strengths and characteristics that evolve and become integral to who we are. From my perspective, this symbolizes all the qualities we should be grateful for; we just need to recognize, appreciate, and utilize them."

Mark then shares another sketch with a different angle of the sculpture and notes, "The back half of the sculpture, still in its unfinished, blocky form, represents our future potential, waiting to be carved, polished, and created. This symbolizes the importance of exercising grace inwardly as we approach and implement areas for future growth. We all have some form of uncarved elements about us. Letting go of the idea that we must always portray ourselves as flawless is liberating. Taking an approach of self-encouragement is empowering. Adopting this mindset can help us cultivate a kind and humble confidence, allowing us to demonstrate the courage to be vulnerable around others. We don't need to seem perfect; we are always in the process of growing. We are all still 'unfinished.'"

Mark and I finish our sandwiches as we wrap up our conversation. As expected, we make plans to return to Lorenzo's next week. I thank Mark for the great discussion. Back at the office, I quickly jot down a few notes:

- Having gratitude for who I am:
  - Enhances my ability to recognize, utilize, and appreciate my worth and capabilities.

- Fosters a humble mindset, keeping me grounded and approachable to others.
- Having grace for who I can be:
  - Creates a safe space for me to embrace growth opportunities, allowing myself to make mistakes and learn from them.
  - Cultivates a kind and humble confidence that reminds me that a perfectionist mindset is unnecessary and that I am still a work in progress. I am still "unfinished."

As I review my notes, I recognize how gratitude and grace illuminate my path forward, affirming that each step—especially the imperfect ones—shapes my growth.

Chapter 7: Generosity – The Key to Core Humility Leadership

That evening, after dinner and putting Addison to bed, Emily and I settle by the fireplace, chatting about our day. She shares her experience speaking to the school's faculty.

"It's funny," Emily says, her face lighting up. "I still get a little nervous before speaking to a large group, even though I've done it dozens of times. But I've learned to let that nervousness shift into excitement once I'm immersed in the moment. There's still a fluttering feeling beforehand, but now I actually look forward to it." I can sense the enthusiasm in her voice.

"That's great," I reply, recalling what Mark shared with me at the office today. "What helped you move from a state of nervousness to enjoyment?"

Emily pauses for a moment, looking at the flames dancing in the fireplace. "I've realized that I don't need to have all the answers. That used to terrify me—I thought that not knowing something would make me seem less credible. I also knew that trying to fake an answer wasn't honest or authentic. Now, when I'm asked a question I don't know the answer to, I simply acknowledge it and say I'll follow up after the presentation. This gives me space to think, and people seem comfortable with that approach. I still prepare thoroughly, but letting go of that pressure has made the entire experience more enjoyable."

"I love that," I say, feeling a wave of recognition. "A few weeks ago at work, I could've used that insight. I felt like I had to know everything, and it made me less effective. I've learned that setting realistic expectations for myself helps me be in a better place to contribute more of what I actually have to offer."

"I totally agree," Emily responds. "It keeps my head clear, enabling me to stay in tune with the audience's needs, rather than wasting energy on worry. So, what did Mark share with you?"

I share with her Mark's story about Michelangelo's unfinished sculpture of Saint Matthew, where the figure appears to be emerging from the stone. He used it to illustrate how gratitude and grace toward ourselves can be transformative. Emily nods, saying she sees how grace helped her create a better speaking environment. She finds it interesting that giving ourselves room to grow can actually accelerate growth more than setting unrealistic expectations.

———

The next morning, amidst back-to-back meetings, I sat down for a follow-up session that Rachel scheduled.

"Having met with my staff to discuss fostering humility internally, do you have any thoughts or new insights you'd like to share?" Rachel asks, clearly interested.

"I certainly do," I reply, eager to share. "Annie, Kristen, and Mark gave me a lot to think about. What they shared truly clarified my perception of leadership. I've been reviewing my notes daily and trying to apply what I've learned. It actually feels pretty natural."

"I agree," Rachel says, her enthusiasm matching mine. "These practices and principles feel natural because they help us see ourselves more clearly and create a safer space to be authentic. I've seen my team apply them effectively, and I knew they'd have valuable insights to share."

She quickly grabs a notepad and writes down the topics her staff discussed with me. I can't help but wonder how this will further develop.

- Recognizing Our Value and Potential
- Embracing Our Unique Approach
- Practicing Gratitude and Grace

"These practices help us stay grounded and clarify who we are," she continues. "They encourage us to use our strengths while developing new ones in a healthy way. So, Ryan, how do you see this affecting how you show up at work?"

I take a moment to reflect. "I feel more like myself," I say. "Emily and I talked last night about how applying humility to ourselves helps quiet anxious thoughts. It allows us to be more present with others. I'm more aware of my strengths—and more willing to explore new ones."

"Love it!" Rachel says. "That authenticity helps us connect with others in a real way. It builds trust."

I realize she's right, as I recall my recent interactions with my team have felt more genuine, and I can sense their trust growing.

Rachel continues, "We've talked about how humility benefits us personally. Doesn't it make sense to apply those same practices and principles to our team?"

I nod, feeling the strength of this insight. "Absolutely. It would feel hypocritical to enjoy the freedom humility brings without applying it and sharing it with others."

"Exactly," she says. "But sometimes our competitive instincts or ideas about success get in the way. Think back to college—how was your success measured?"

"By outperforming others," I admit. "Higher scores meant better grades."

"And your first job?" she presses.

"The same concept applied: improved performance led to bigger salary increases," I note.

"Now that you are a senior manager, it's important for your mindset to evolve. Your team's results are now even more important than your individual achievements. One key trait that can help with this transition is generosity. Before we explore this further, I'd like to show you a video about hummingbirds that illustrates this point. Have you ever watched hummingbirds at a feeder?" Rachel asks.

"I have," I reply, curiosity piqued.

"They're fascinating creatures," she says. "I recently learned more about them. These tiny birds live across North, Central, and South America, as well as the Caribbean. Their wings beat incredibly fast—between 50 to 80 times per second—which means they burn through energy quickly. To keep going, they need to consume nectar from flowers or the sweet liquid people put in feeders."

She pulls up a short video on her tablet. "Watch this."

The video features two hummingbirds surrounded by several feeders, each filled with ample nectar to sustain them for weeks. But instead of feeding, one bird spends all its energy chasing the other away from every feeder. In the end, neither bird drinks.

Rachel pauses the video. "What do you make of that?"

"It's clear," I respond quickly. "The aggressive bird was so focused on keeping the other bird away. Neither is strengthened nor benefits from the feeders."

"Do you see similar behavior in the work environment?" asked Rachel.

I ponder on this question and come to a recognition, "In the office, this type of behavior can occur when we think we're looking out for our own self-interest—hoarding information or withholding credit—under the belief that it increases our value. In reality, it drains our energies and fosters a distrustful work environment."

"Exactly," Rachel says. "That behavior is instinctive for birds—it's hardwired for survival. However, as individuals, we have a choice. When we operate from that same survival mindset, it can become unhealthy, as we've seen in both the hummingbirds and the examples you shared."

She leans in slightly. "As leaders, our responsibilities extend beyond self-preservation. We're here to help sustain others—to support their growth, development, and success. That means coaching, sharing, and allowing others to shine. Ultimately, it all comes back to generosity—the quality of being plentiful.

"Author Stephen R. Covey describes this as the 'abundance mentality'—a belief that there is plenty out there and enough to spare for everyone. He explains that this mindset flows from a deep sense of personal worth and security."

Rachel picks up a marker and draws a circle on the whiteboard. The lower half is shaded light brown and divided into four segments: Value, Uniqueness, Gratitude, and Grace. The upper half is shaded green and labeled Generosity.

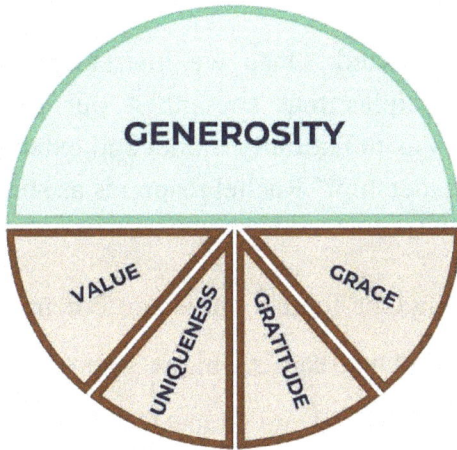

"I had you meet with my staff to explore how these four lower segments shown here help us gain clearer self-perception and feel safer being our authentic selves. Notice that the segments of the lower semicircle in this drawing are light brown or earth tone, representing the ground. These four areas provide us with stability and encourage us to stay grounded, as humility teaches. As we cultivate humility internally, it can naturally lead to generosity towards others, including our team members."

She taps the green upper semicircle. "Generosity is highlighted in green. It is positioned above the earth or ground area of the lower semicircle. This placement above the ground symbolizes that generosity enables our desire and ability to 'grow others' and support their development. It involves giving benefits to others without expecting anything in return. Without generosity, our focus tend to turn inwards, which is a poor quality in leadership.

"For simplicity, I call this the Humility Circle. It is an easy reminder for me to remain grounded and to help grow others," remarks Rachel.

I reflect on this and then ask, "So, how can I apply generosity in my leadership approach?"

"I'm glad you asked. Once we internalize the foundational practices and principles that strengthen our personal humility, generosity enables us to naturally model and extend these qualities to others in our leadership," Rachel responds as she notes:

- Recognizing Our Team's Value and Potential
- Encouraging Our Team's Unique Approach
- Extending Gratitude and Grace Toward Our Team

"As you know, we have our staff off-site event coming up this Friday, and I promise it will be a great event. I plan to dedicate part of our meeting to discussing how to implement these principles in our leadership approach. This is a wonderful opportunity for all of us to reflect on our experiences and consider our goals for future growth and development. I will also have the other staff members share their insights on these topics, so you won't have to listen to me the entire time," Rachel jokes. "I'll give them a heads-up to prepare their thoughts."

"I'm looking forward to it," I reply, feeling excited about the upcoming discussions. It is refreshing to be on a team that values such open dialogue on topics like this. Back at my desk, I made a few notes from our conversation:

- Generosity—The quality of being plentiful.
- Thinking about Rachel's Humility Circle drawing:
  - Lower Semicircle— "Earth" representing having my feet firmly on the ground. These practices and principles help me internalize humility. This foundation provides me with stability and inspires a natural generosity towards my team.
  - Upper Semicircle—The green area above the "earth" symbolized how generosity grows from that foundation, increasing my desire and ability to develop others by modeling and practicing humility toward my team.

As I reflect on my recent experiences as a developing leader, I'm eager to share insights that could foster meaningful discussions at our offsite on Friday. My goal is to enhance our time together and make a positive contribution to our team.

Chapter 8: Applying Core Humility Leadership Towards Others

It's Friday, and excitement is in the air as our staff off-site event unfolds at the stunning conference center nestled within our town's picturesque golf course. Rachel has gone above and beyond, orchestrating a round of golf for us immediately after the meeting—a perfect blend of work and play. She's encouraged everyone to wear their casual golf attire, promising a day that's not only about business but also about bonding.

As we gather for breakfast, the atmosphere is filled with anticipation. The aroma of freshly baked pastries fills the room, inviting us to indulge in the delightful spread that awaits. Chilled glasses of freshly squeezed juices and smoothies enhance our morning meal. Conversations shift from work plans to weekend activities. It's nice to connect with the team in this relaxed setting before a day of golf. The sun shines outside, promising pleasant weather for the game—a terrific way to start the weekend.

After breakfast, we dive into a discussion about our vision for the team a year from now. It's a creative exercise that feels particularly vital for me as I'm still getting to know everyone and trying to understand our collective direction. Afterward, Rachel invites the senior managers to share how they demonstrate elements of humility toward their teams.

"Since Ryan is new to our staff," Rachel begins, "I thought this would be a perfect opportunity to revisit one of my favorite topics: leadership humility. Thank you, Annie, Kristen, and Mark, for meeting with Ryan over the past few weeks to discuss the importance of internalizing the supporting practices and principles of Core Humility. Just a few days ago, Ryan and I explored the principle of generosity, and I'd like to build on that today. I appreciate your willingness to share what's helped you apply this to your teams. I've asked each of you to present just one slide to keep things focused. Annie, would you like to kick us off?"

"Absolutely," Annie replies without missing a beat. "Ryan and I recently talked about recognizing our individual value and potential. Today, I want to share what I've learned about recognizing my team's value and potential."

She clicks to display a photo of her niece's baseball team on the screen.

"This picture reminds me how I can actively practice humility towards my team. You'll notice the coaches in the background. I've seen different coaching styles—some focus on using only their best players to win. In contrast, others prioritize giving everyone a chance to play, even if it means sacrificing short-term victories. I won't say which approach is best, as I recognize that it depends on the circumstances. In this case, I appreciated how my niece's coaches emphasized developing each player's skills rather than simply focusing on winning. They weren't seeking the spotlight; they were focused on the team's individual growth. That created an environment my niece genuinely enjoys. So, how do you think this applies to us and our teams today?"

"I've learned that leadership requires being more outward-focused," Kristen responds. "When I first became a manager, that shift was huge. Like you said, Annie, I realized I needed to shine the spotlight on my team instead of myself. Their success had to matter more than mine—not just for them, but for our collective team."

"Didn't that feel like you were achieving less personally?" I ask, genuinely curious about her perspective.

Kristen smiles. "I'll answer that by building on Annie's analogy. How many home runs does a good coach hit during a game?"

I think for a moment, the answer clicks into place. "None— they're not the ones batting."

"Exactly," Annie agrees passionately. "And does the coach need to be the best pitcher or batter?"

"Not necessarily," I reply.

"As a coach, it's actually a strength to have team members whose skills exceed our own," Annie emphasizes. "That applies to our roles at FutureGen, too. A generous mindset toward my team empowers me to confidently recognize and value the strengths each member brings. With that awareness, I'm able to delegate with intention, matching assignments to individual capabilities and fostering an environment where each person can thrive.

"I didn't always think this way. But I've come to realize that when my team excels, it doesn't diminish my worth—it enhances our collective value and impact. By letting go of comparisons, I can better see and support their growth. It's less about the potential of 'me' and more about the potential of 'we.'

"I love the work of Stephen M. R. Covey, who emphasizes that leaders who are secure and credible are not threatened by the success of others. In his book *The Speed of Trust*, he explains that when we operate from a place of inner security, we can genuinely celebrate others' strengths and contributions. This mindset builds trust, strengthens relationships, and ultimately elevates the performance of the entire team.

"By embracing this mindset, leadership becomes less about proving my value and more about unlocking the potential of those around me, which is crucial in today's fast-paced environment."

"Thank you, Annie," Rachel says thoughtfully. "Helping our team members reach their full potential is a core leadership responsibility. It takes humility to let go of comparisons and support others in their excellence. Ultimately, that mindset improves how we perceive and care for our staff—and helps us coach them to hit home runs for the team."

After a quick 10-minute break, we reconvene for our next topic: Encouraging Our Team's Unique Approach. Kristen leads the discussion and shares a slide of a snowboarder with an embedded video of an Olympic event.

"What I love about generosity in relation to humility," Kristen begins with a feeling of clarity, "is that while I may have a specific way of tackling challenges, it's important to encourage others to take their own approach. Unless we're asking for help, it's rarely enjoyable when someone dictates exactly how to do something. I value having the freedom to determine my own path, and I want to give others that same freedom. It allows them to thrive.

"I want to share a video about an Olympic gold medalist snowboarder named Ester Ledecka. What makes this video particularly interesting is that Ester is competing in a skiing event, which is quite different from her sport of snowboarding. She decided to take on a new challenge by entering the Super-G skiing event at the 2018 Olympics in South Korea. She qualified for the race but was ranked so low that by the time the top 20 qualified skiers finished, most media coverage had already moved on to other events before her turn. Most people believed they already knew the winner would be Anna Veith of Austria. As the day progressed, it was Ester's turn to compete. Just before the race, she even broke part of her ski boot!"

Kristen then starts the video. As we watch Ester ski down the mountain, we see her elapsed time displayed as she races through the course. Something unexpected happens: partway down the mountain, her progress time is highlighted in green, indicating that she has the fastest time at each checkpoint. The backup media announcers seem stunned as they observe her performance. Everyone focuses intently on the clock as Ester soars over the final stretch of the course. Upon crossing the finish line, her time remains highlighted in green. She has just won the event by a mere 0.01 seconds, securing the gold medal. However, she appears confused when informed of her victory, insisting that there must be some kind of mistake and that they need to add more time to her total. Once it becomes clear to her that she has won, she graciously accepts the result, demonstrating humility and strength in the face of a surprise victory.

"So, how do you think Ester Ledecka's approach contributed to her victory in this event?" asks Kristen.

"I think she felt less pressure than the other competitors," Mark replies. "That probably gave her the freedom to navigate the slope in her own unique way."

"Maybe her snowboarding background gave her an edge," I add. "She might've found a slightly better line down the course."

"Great insights," Kristen says. "How can we apply this to our teams?"

"They may have effective ways to reach goals that differ from ours," I add. "We should give them space to explore."

"Exactly," Kristen replies. "The goal of the Olympic event was the same for everyone: finish the course in the shortest time while following the rules. But how they got there was up to them. When team members feel empowered to forge their own paths—within safe and ethical boundaries—they can draw on their experiences and creativity to find better solutions. That process builds confidence and teaches valuable lessons. There's real satisfaction in discovering a solution and knowing you played a key role in it."

Rachel thanks Kristen for her insights and calls for a 15-minute break. We grab refreshments and head to the patio to enjoy the sunshine, joking about our upcoming golf game and downplaying our skills.

After the break, Rachel hands the floor to Mark, who speaks about the importance of extending gratitude and grace to our team. He shares the same sketches of Michelangelo's Saint Matthew that he showed me earlier in the week during his recent trip to Florence.

"As I mentioned to Ryan," Mark begins, "this unfinished sculpture reminds me not only of how I should treat myself, but also of how I should see and treat others. The mostly completed front represents each team member's current development—the strengths I can appreciate in them right now. In contrast, the sculpture's rough, unfinished back half symbolizes my team member's future potential, reminding me to extend grace as I support them in nurturing and cultivating that potential.

"Earlier in my career, my manager was modeling this aspect of humility in how he treated me, though I didn't fully realize it at the time. I worked at a manufacturing company where I collaborated with a vendor to design instrument modules for our product. After I approved the design, the vendor built the module. The finished module arrived while I was on vacation, and the factory attempted to install and test it. Guess what? It didn't work; it didn't even power up. I learned about this while traveling back home from our trip. I felt sick to my stomach the entire way home and feared I would lose my job.

"When I met with my manager the next day, I was bracing myself for the worst. I apologized for the mistake, and to my surprise, he said encouragingly, 'Get over it, Mark! You and the team will work together to find a solution and get us back on track.'

"I was stunned and couldn't believe how supportive my manager was. Guess what happened next? His support gave me the confidence I desperately needed to move forward. After investigating with our team, we discovered an error in the product's interface drawing. The solution turned out to be surprisingly simple, and I gained a valuable perspective that allowed me to view others in a more supportive and empathetic light. That project challenged me greatly, and my manager used it as a pivotal opportunity to help me grow and develop. Perhaps he anticipated that there would be some bumps along the way and saw those challenges as a chance to build my skills. I'll never forget that experience."

"I can't imagine how differently things might have turned out if your manager had responded the way you originally expected, Mark," Annie says. "The outcome would have been quite different for both of you."

"Exactly," Mark replies. "Because he thought long-term, we built a stronger relationship. I knew he truly had my back.

"Expressing gratitude to our team members involves acknowledging and valuing their accomplishments. Being generous helps us notice and appreciate their positive contributions, especially during challenging times. As Annie implied earlier, we're not competing against our team; instead, we're rooting for their success.

"And grace? How do you think my former manager applied this to me?"

I pause momentarily and respond, "Your manager gave you the safety and space to take on that daunting project. As you noted, he probably expected mistakes to happen but saw them as part of your growth."

"Yes, having that vision in advance allowed him to respond with a long-term perspective," Mark shares.

"And a single mistake doesn't define a person," Rachel interjected. "It's vital to help people learn from their mistakes. We should focus on helping rather than punishing. They may feel overwhelmed by their errors, but just like Mark experienced, we can be supportive of their growth opportunities when they need it most."

After Mark offers closing comments on his topic, Rachel moves on to wrap up our meeting.

"Thank you all for sharing and participating in this timely discussion of how you actively apply humility toward your team," Rachel says as she displays the topics we covered on the screen:

- Recognizing Our Team's Value and Potential
- Encouraging Our Team's Unique Approach
- Extending Gratitude and Grace to Our Team

Rachel then shares our final slide of the day. The Humility Circle, as she calls it:

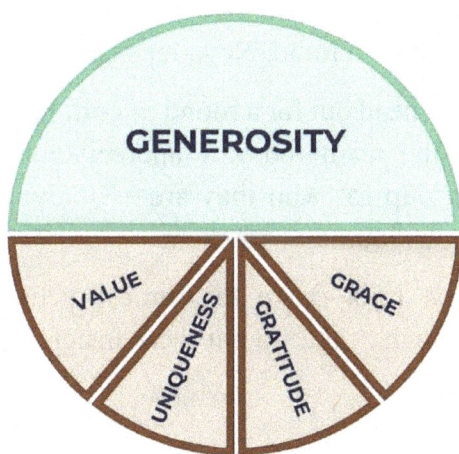

Rachel continues, "As we build a solid foundation of humility internally, noted in the light brown or earth-toned section of this familiar drawing, it helps us see ourselves more clearly and feel safe being authentic. Having our feet firmly on the ground in this manner can foster a sense of generosity towards others, helping us desire to see everyone be successful. This generosity, illustrated in the green semicircle, naturally guides us to behave as we discussed today with our team members. This encapsulates what I envision as our key leadership approach. The green section of the graphic symbolizes our desire to nurture the growth of our team members, enabling them to reach their full potential. We are in our current leadership roles for their benefit."

"So, what do you see as our next steps?" Annie asks, leaning forward with interest.

"Great question," Rachel replies, her tone bright with enthusiasm. "To honor the spirit of encouraging your unique approach, I'd like each of you to decide how you'll apply these practices within your teams. Take time to reflect, craft a plan, and implement it in a way that aligns with your style. This isn't just a discussion—it's a call to action. Expect some learning along the way; leaders need grace, too. I'd love for us to share our experiences soon, so let's keep that in mind. Now, let's eat—lunch is here!"

After lunch, we head out for a round of golf. I genuinely enjoyed connecting with the team today. I appreciate Rachel and each member of our group for who they are as individuals, and I feel grateful to be on this journey with them.

Later that day, I jot down the three practices for applying humility toward others, eager to put these insights into action right away:

- Recognizing Our Team's Value and Potential
  - Let go of the need to be in the spotlight. Shine it on the team. Coach the team to hit home runs.

- Encouraging Our Team's Unique Approach
  - Empower my team to take their own approach while staying within the appropriate boundaries of safety and ethics. This enables my team to engage in the creative process and build the confidence they need to face new challenges.

- Extending Gratitude and Grace to Our Team
  - Create a safe environment for my team to tackle new challenges and learn from their experiences, including mistakes, in a positive manner.

As I finish my notes, a surge of responsibility washes over me. With Rachel's encouragement echoing in my mind, I realize it's my turn to take the lead. Tasked with creating the action plan she requested, I'm eager to transform these insights into tangible steps for my team. Now, the challenge is not only to envision but also to execute—it's time to turn our discussions into impactful actions.

Chapter 9: My Plan

This weekend, I've set aside time for self-reflection, inspired by Rachel's thoughtful invitation to bring the practices and principles of Core Humility into the fabric of my team's dynamics. I genuinely appreciate her encouragement for each of us to develop our own unique plans. So, on a bit of a whim, I decide to head to the local park, looking for a peaceful spot to soak in the sunlight and enjoy the fresh air while I start to sketch out my thoughts.

As I review my notes from the past few weeks, I begin to see a web of interconnected ideas emerging that illuminate my thinking. I recall my early conversations with Rachel; they were pivotal moments that helped initiate my understanding of what humility truly means. This realization emphasized the importance of self-awareness, which is crucial for genuinely incorporating humility into my leadership style:

- Humility means being grounded:
    - Having my feet firmly planted. Being self-aware, authentic, and steady—leading from a place of clarity and internalized core values.
    - It's not inflating nor diminishing who I am.
    - It's not placing myself above or below others.
    - It's about wearing my own shoes.
- To see my "whole self," I need to acknowledge both my strengths and challenges simultaneously.
- Wearing a "mask" to hide my perceived shortcomings prevents others from seeing the full extent of who I am and drains my mental energy in the process.

These insights reinforce the importance of being authentic with my team. When I try to be anything else, it feels insincere and likely undermines their trust.

From my session with Annie on recognizing my value and potential, I noted:

- Humility includes utilizing all of my strengths—they're part of my authentic self.
- Challenges have value. I don't need to broadcast or feel embarrassed by them. Instead, I can see them as future opportunities and tools for growth.
- A clear self-awareness enables me to cultivate humility and helps me remain teachable.

These reflections motivate me to present my best self to my team, not to show off, but to uplift and support each member. I understand that as I build credibility with my team, I can openly share aspects of my leadership journey with them, doing so with confident vulnerability.

Regarding the importance of embracing my unique approach, my session notes with Kristen reinforce the following:

- Each of us is running our own unique race, with individual strengths and challenges. Embracing my unique approach is both healthy and empowering.

- Comparing myself to others consumes valuable mental energy. It can prevent me from being my authentic self and distract me from self-awareness.

- I can cultivate a more productive and positive mindset by celebrating the successes of others.

In this session, I discovered the value of embracing my unique leadership style with my team, rather than imitating others, a trap I had unknowingly fallen into in the past. It's empowering to recognize the strides I'm making on my journey to becoming a better leader. Instead of measuring myself against others, I'm choosing to focus on my own growth and evolution.

What's even more enlightening is the realization that celebrating the achievements of my colleagues doesn't diminish my own worth; instead, it amplifies it and fosters a collaborative spirit within the team. This shift in perspective is enriching not only for me but for the entire group, creating an environment where we can all thrive together.

I review my session notes with Mark, where we discussed practicing gratitude and grace:

- Having gratitude for who I am:
  - Enhances my ability to recognize, utilize, and appreciate my worth and capabilities.
  - Fosters a humble mindset, keeping me grounded and approachable to others.
- Having grace for who I can be:
  - Creates a safe space for me to embrace growth opportunities, allowing myself to make mistakes and learn from them.
  - Cultivates a kind and humble confidence that reminds me that a perfectionist mindset is unnecessary and that I am still a work in progress. I am still "unfinished."

I deeply appreciate the focus of this session on self-encouragement and fostering a growth mindset. It creates an empowering atmosphere where I feel safe to challenge myself and pursue personal improvement. Whenever I stumble or encounter a mistake, I can remember to cut myself some slack, transforming those moments into invaluable opportunities for growth. This perspective lightens the pressure of seeking perfection in front of my team and peers.

The three sessions I participated in with my peers, each centered on embracing humility, proved especially eye-opening. They allowed me to gain deeper insights into who I am and the unique contributions I bring to the table. I've come to recognize that I possess a distinct blend of skills and tools that can contribute to my team's success. With this newfound clarity, I can confidently embrace my own style of effective leadership.

I review the Humility Circle sketch that Rachel made:

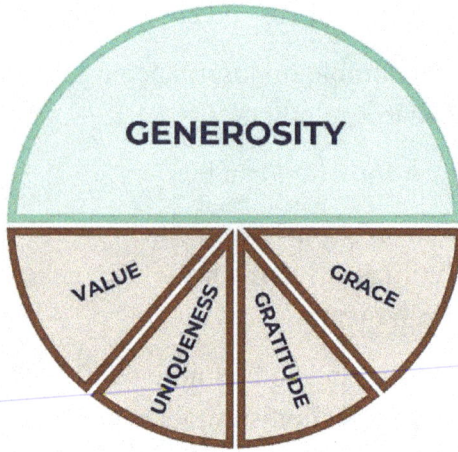

The lower semicircle in this sketch serves as a vivid reminder of the vital importance of staying grounded—being self-aware, authentic, and steady—never placing myself above or below others. The four practices and principles outlined here intricately weave humility into my character, shaping how I interact with those around me. They fuel my desire to be generous toward others, captured by the green semicircle that emphasizes my commitment to nurturing the growth of my colleagues and team.

VALUE

Back at the office on Monday, a buzz of excitement courses through me. I'm ready to put my newly learned practices into action. My first meeting is with Aaron in the morning, followed by a session with Sarah after lunch.

As I prepare for Aaron's meeting, I can't help but reflect on his expertise in Organizational Change Management (OCM). Thanks to Annie's insights, I remind myself that I don't need to feel threatened by his strengths. In coaching, it's not about being the best; it's about empowering others to reach their full potential. So, how can I effectively coach Aaron? What growth opportunities can I help him uncover?

When Aaron walks in and gives his project update, I feel a sense of ease settle over me—I'm genuinely excited about his talent. As the sole OCM specialist juggling multiple projects, he confides that he's overwhelmed.

"Thanks for sharing, Aaron. Can you elaborate on how this challenge is affecting your workload?" I ask.

"I want to excel in all my projects," he admits. "But lately, I've been stuck in endless meetings and can't find the time to create and implement needed OCM plans. I have the skills, but I need more hours in the day. If only I had a clone!"

"So, you've got the capability, but there's only one of you. How else could you leverage your expertise?" I ask, eager to help him see the possibilities.

"I could create training materials for project managers to manage some OCM responsibilities," he reflects, his mind visibly churning. "I'd act as a consultant, assigning tasks they could take on independently. That would free me up for more specialized work."

"I've seen your fantastic training plans. What about teaching this as a class?" I suggest, curious if he'd considered this before.

Aaron pauses, a slight smile on his face. "I've developed many training modules, but I've never actually been the one to instruct. It's always been the stakeholders who deliver the training. However, maybe I could be the 'voice' for this content, at least for the OCM class. That would really broaden my impact."

"I think you just figured out how to clone yourself," I joke, watching as his face lights up at the thought.

With renewed energy, he starts formulating a plan for outlining the class content and even considers enrolling in a facilitation skills class to enhance his public speaking abilities.

We wrap up the meeting on a high note—a stark contrast to our first encounter when I felt nervous and intimidated. This time, I see myself in a new light—as a coach. I'm grateful for Aaron's talents, and my goal now is to help him achieve his best performance and encourage further growth.

After a quick lunch, I prepare myself for my meeting with Sarah, our dynamic senior project manager who spearheads the Advanced Manufacturing Integration (AMI) project. I can't help but reflect on her recent success in guiding her team through a major hurdle they faced with their testing data. Instead of suggesting they slog through longer hours, as was my initial thought, Sarah took a bold approach. She encouraged her team to hit pause and dive deep into the root cause of their issue.

This is my opportunity to implement the lesson Kristen shared—encouraging our team to pursue their own unique approach. I glance through my notes, reminding myself of the power in granting team members the freedom to carve their own paths within safe and ethical boundaries. That autonomy builds confidence and lays the groundwork for invaluable lessons.

As the meeting approaches, Sarah arrives, her voice brimming with enthusiasm. "We're back on schedule!" she beams, revealing how her team has rallied after overcoming recent obstacles. Just weeks ago, tensions simmered among members, but resolving the corrupt data issue transformed not just their work but their camaraderie.

Intrigued, I press Sarah for insight into this shift. "It was a game-changer," she explains. "The team faced a problem that impacted us all, uniting us with a common purpose. Initially, they were frustrated when I asked them to halt testing, worried it would push back our timeline even further. But I encouraged brainstorming to figure out what was going wrong.

"That's when one team member made a pivotal observation. As I mentioned the other day, while we were focused on fixing bugs in the code, we had unquestioningly trusted that our test data was accurate. The question was – what if the data was flawed? Taking that seriously, our test engineer dove into the investigation. She discovered serious corruption in the data source and quickly created a new, accurate dataset for our team to use.

"Surprisingly, this challenge brought us closer together and I'm thankful it happened; it helped us bond, boost morale, and elevate our productivity."

"You epitomize what Kristen emphasized about empowering teams to pursue solutions they create," I respond. "Your approach not only uplifted their spirits but made a tangible impact."

She smiles, grateful for the affirmation. As we delve deeper into our conversation, Sarah opens up about new challenges looming over another project. A wave of gratitude washes over me—I can sense the trust building between us as she seeks my input. Her urgency is evident, and I can tell she's eager for a collaborative brainstorming session.

I threw out a few thought-provoking questions for her to consider, and she quickly formulates a plan as we jointly consider the matter.

As we wrap up, I realize Sarah walks away feeling empowered and capable, retaining ownership of her path forward in addressing the current challenges. I merely needed to ask the right questions to guide her thinking. This experience is yet another powerful reminder that as a leader, my role is not necessarily to give answers, but to inspire and nurture my team's ability to create solutions.

GRATITUDE

GRACE

Later that afternoon, Sean stops by my office with a sense of urgency in his demeanor. I motion for him to take a seat, feeling that something serious is weighing on him. His team has just signed the contract for the OptiChain software, a crucial element of the Supply Chain Optimization (SCO) project he is leading. However, it's clear that something is unsettling him.

"We need to talk," he starts without any preamble. "We're gearing up for our kickoff meeting with the vendor, but they just swapped out several of their key team members who we thought would be on this project. We raised our concerns with their lead, but she mentioned they had to 'restructure' some of their internal teams. When we insisted on the original team, she hit us with the contract fine print that allows for these changes. I checked myself—there's nothing in there that bars it."

I take a moment to digest this. The situation is frustrating, but I remember the lessons Mark taught me about gratitude and grace. Sean is a valuable asset to our team, and this moment, though challenging, presents an opportunity for him to learn and grow. The complexity of his project only amplifies the stakes, and I want to support him through these turbulent waters.

"Thank you for sharing this with me, Sean," I reply, genuinely empathizing. "I can see how maddening this must be. There's an expectation, almost an implicit agreement, that the team you negotiate with will be the one you work with after the contract is signed. This gives us a valuable learning opportunity. How do you think you'd handle this differently next time?"

A flicker of relief washes over Sean as we shift the focus to the "next time."

"I'd make sure we include terms in the contract that require our approval for any vendor staff changes," he replies, his determination growing.

"That's a solid idea," I nod. "A lot of what we include in our vendor contracts comes from past experiences, both good and bad."

To empower him further, I ask, "What can you do right now to keep this project on track despite this matter? What do you still have control over?"

A realization dawns, "Although they won't change the contract terms, they have indicated multiple times that they would like us to act as a reference for their company. This is something we can influence.

"I will communicate our high expectations for the timely and budget-conscious completion of this project. I will emphasize that our potential as a strong reference is directly linked to their success. Additionally, I'll highlight the fact that we will be monitoring their progress closely to ensure they meet all contractual requirements.

"I will make it clear that if their revised team encounters any setbacks in meeting the contract requirements, we expect them to quickly involve the necessary individuals to help us get back on track. It is important that they maintain this direction until the project is complete," Sean states.

"With the options we have available, that sounds like an excellent game plan, Sean. Setting high expectations and ensuring accountability will definitely help. I also like your strategy of tying their success to our willingness to be a reference," I affirm, genuinely impressed.

Now visibly reenergized, Sean responds, "Thanks, Ryan. I'm feeling much better about this. I have a meeting with the vendor tomorrow, and I'll be sure to keep you posted on how it goes."

"Absolutely, I look forward to your update," I say with a smile. "By the way, when is our next golf putting derby?"

A sly look appears on Sean's face. "This Friday at lunchtime! Are you ready for the competition? It's going to be intense," he quips.

"Count me in. This is going to be fun." I reply. I'm genuinely looking forward to this event.

As we conclude our discussion, I realize that my interaction with Sean was far more productive than I initially expected. Our conversation has truly strengthened our working relationship. I reflect on Mark's insightful advice about providing others with the safety and space to challenge themselves—something Sean has certainly done by leading this complex project. It's also essential to help them learn and grow through their experiences.

—

That evening, my parents come over to celebrate Addison's first birthday. After dinner, we gather in the family room to help her open gifts. We laugh as she seems more interested in chewing the wrapping paper than the presents.

"So, Ryan, now you're a senior manager at FutureGen!" my father remarks. "I hope you're enjoying the responsibility of being a leader. You know, I had plenty of experience with that when I was my company's vice president of sales."

I couldn't help chuckling a bit when my dad pointed this out. He had a successful career and took pride in letting people know that he was a vice president whenever the opportunity arose. As Addison searched for more wrapping paper to chew on, I said, "I must admit, Dad, this new position was challenging for me at first. I struggled to behave in the way I thought a leader should. Fortunately, my new director also happens to be an excellent mentor. Over the past three weeks, she and her team have shared important practices and principles for incorporating humility into my leadership approach.

"In this short time, what they have taught me has helped me feel more grounded as I strive to be my authentic self. This shift has lifted the burden I had placed on myself by trying to act like the kind of leader I thought I was supposed to be. Now, I appreciate the value I bring and the natural contributions I can offer to others. I also have a greater appreciation for the value that others contribute. It's been an incredible journey, and I now see leadership in a new light—it's less about being in charge and more about cultivating the greatness within my team."

"That's an interesting approach, Ryan. I wonder how it would have worked in my day," my father questions.

"I believe it would have worked well, Dad. The more I learn about the principles of leadership and humility, the more I realize that these concepts have been around for a long time. People just stray from them occasionally," I reply.

"Speaking of things that never change," Emily remarks as she looks at her phone, "Uncle Brian just texted that the Net Rangers are ready for another 'Challenge Round' this Monday evening."

"Net Rangers? Challenge Round?" my mom asks. "That sounds just like my brother Brian. When we were kids and played board games, he would suddenly shout, 'Challenge Round!' This meant the winner would receive some sort of prize, like a piece of candy or a coin."

"Yes, Mom. Yet another example of things that never change," I replied. "Emily, if you're good with this, can you tell Uncle Brian we gladly accept the Net Rangers challenge?"

"Already have, Ryan! Already have!" Emily grinned.

YOUR PLAN

Chapter 10: Your Plan

Thank you for taking the time to read *Core Humility – A Story of Leadership Authenticity*. I genuinely hope that your journey with humility not only enriches your life but also has a positive impact on the lives of those around you. Engaging with the concepts of humility can lead to profound personal growth and deeper relationships with others.

After finishing a self-help book, I often find myself searching for effective ways to retain and apply the new ideas I've learned. I invite you to do the same. It is through active reflection and application of these insights that true transformation occurs.

To help you internalize the principles shared in *Core Humility*, I encourage you to take a closer look at the insights provided by our friend Ryan. Chapter 10 serves as a concise summary of the key principles discussed in the earlier chapters. This chapter is designed to prompt you to reflect critically and consider how to weave these valuable ideas into your character and daily life.

Each section in this chapter includes vital points and thought-provoking questions to help you outline your personal growth plan. I recommend setting aside some quiet time to reflect on these questions and jot down your thoughts. This reflection will not only help clarify your understanding but also enhance your commitment to practicing humility.

As you begin to apply these concepts, I hope you will discover more about yourself and uncover the potential that lies within. Embracing humility can open doors to new opportunities, foster empathy, and build stronger connections with others.

Thank you for reading my book. May your path of humility be enlightening and empowering, leading you toward an even more fulfilling and meaningful journey.

Please review the following pages as you formulate Your Plan.

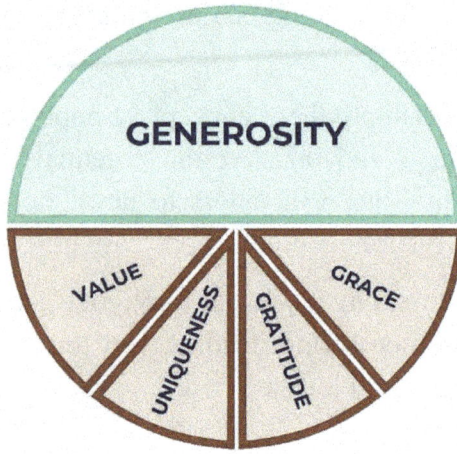

Humility and a Clear Self-Awareness (Ch. 2-3):

- Humility means being grounded:
  - Having my feet firmly planted. Being self-aware, authentic, and steady—leading from a place of clarity and internalized core values.
  - It's not inflating nor diminishing who I am.
  - It's not placing myself above or below others.
  - It's about wearing my own shoes.
- To see my "whole self," I need to acknowledge both my strengths and challenges simultaneously.
- Wearing a "mask" to hide my perceived shortcomings prevents others from seeing the full extent of who I am and drains my mental energy in the process.

Questions for Reader:

Are there areas where I could embrace my authentic self more fully?

Are there any masks I could consider removing?

_____

_____

_____

_____

_____

_____

_____

_____

_____

_____

_____

_____

_____

_____

_____

_____

VALUE

Recognizing My Value and Potential (Ch. 4):

- Humility includes utilizing all of my strengths—they're part of my authentic self.

- Challenges have value. I don't need to broadcast or feel embarrassed by them. Instead, I can see them as future opportunities and tools for growth.

- A clear self-awareness enables me to cultivate humility and helps me remain teachable.

Questions for Reader:

What strengths can I utilize more fully?

What challenges can I focus on to become stronger? Who can I share this with?

_____

_____

_____

_____

_____

_____

_____

_____

_____

_____

_____

_____

_____

_____

_____

_____

_____

_____

Embracing My Own Unique Approach (Ch. 5):

- Each of us is running our own unique race, with individual strengths and challenges. Embracing my unique approach is both healthy and empowering.

- Comparing myself to others consumes valuable mental energy. It can prevent me from being my authentic self and distract me from self-awareness.

- I can cultivate a more productive and positive mindset by celebrating the successes of others.

Questions for Reader:

Is there a part of my job or life that would benefit from applying my own unique approach even more?

How can I enjoy my own path more instead of comparing myself to others?

How can I adopt a more generous attitude toward those around me?

_____

_____

_____

_____

_____

_____

_____

_____

_____

_____

_____

_____

_____

_____

_____

Practicing Gratitude and Grace (Ch. 6):

- Having gratitude for who I am:
  - Enhances my ability to recognize, utilize, and appreciate my worth and capabilities.
  - Fosters a humble mindset, keeping me grounded and approachable to others.
- Having grace for who I can be:
  - Creates a safe space for me to embrace growth opportunities, allowing myself to make mistakes and learn from them.
  - Cultivates a kind and humble confidence that reminds me that a perfectionist mindset is unnecessary and that I am still a work in progress. I am still "unfinished."

Question for Reader:

What is my next growth opportunity, knowing I'll give myself "permission" to learn along the way?

_____

_____

_____

_____

_____

_____

_____

_____

_____

_____

_____

_____

_____

_____

_____

_____

_____

_____

GENEROSITY

Recognizing My Team's Value and Potential (Chapter 8):

- Let go of the need to be in the spotlight. Shine it on the team. Coach the team to hit home runs.

Questions for Reader:

What practices can I implement to better identify my team's strengths?

How can I effectively coach them toward reaching their next stage of growth?

_____

_____

_____

_____

_____

_____

_____

_____

_____

_____

_____

_____

_____

_____

_____

_____

GENEROSITY

Encouraging My Team's Unique Approach (Chapter 8)

- Empower my team to take their own approach while staying within the appropriate boundaries of safety and ethics. This enables my team to engage in the creative process and build the confidence they need to face new challenges.

Question for Reader:

What practices can I implement to encourage my team members to tackle challenges using their unique approaches?

_____

_____

_____

_____

_____

_____

_____

_____

_____

_____

_____

_____

_____

_____

_____

_____

_____

GENEROSITY

Extending Gratitude and Grace to My Team (Chapter 8):

- Create a safe environment for my team to tackle new challenges and learn from their experiences, including mistakes, in a positive manner.

Questions for Reader:

How can I create a safe environment that empowers my team members to take on new challenges?

How can I help my team members learn constructively from their experiences?

_____

_____

_____

_____

_____

_____

_____

_____

_____

_____

_____

_____

_____

_____

_____

I'd love to hear how these principles impact you and about your journey. Please visit my website, AuthentureCoaching.com, or email me at klavering@gmail.com to share your stories.

Thank you again,

Kevin Lavering

References

[1] O'Connell, B. (2021, May 18). *Hail to the 'Humble' Manager.* SHRM. https://www.shrm.org/topics-tools/news/managing-smart/hail-to-humble-manager

[2] Palmer, Parker J. *Let Your Life Speak: Listening for the Voice of Vocation.* San Francisco: Jossey-Bass, 1999, p. 70.

[3] Herrity, Jennifer. "What Is Self-Awareness? (And How To Increase Yours)." *Indeed Career Guide*, March 26, 2025. https://www.indeed.com/career-advice/career-development/what-is-self-awareness

[4] Lencioni, Patrick. *The Ideal Team Player: How to Recognize and Cultivate the Three Essential Virtues*. San Francisco: Jossey-Bass, 2016, p. 158.

[5] Friedland, Daniel. *Leading Well from Within: A Neuroscience and Mindfulness-Based Framework for Conscious Leadership*. Self-published, 2016, p. 92.

[6,7] Covey, Stephen R. *The 7 Habits of Highly Effective People: Powerful Lessons in Personal Change.* Revised ed., Simon & Schuster, 2020, pp. 82–83, 219–221.

[8] Covey, S. M. R. *The Speed of Trust: The One Thing That Changes Everything*. Simon & Schuster, 2008, p. 238.

About the Author

Kevin Lavering is a seasoned program director, instructor, conference speaker, and a passionate advocate for authentic, people-centered leadership. With decades of experience guiding teams through complex projects and organizational change, Kevin has learned that the most enduring influence comes not from authority but from humility, generosity, and the courage to lead with integrity.

Throughout his career, Kevin has helped both emerging and experienced leaders discover their unique strengths and lead with greater clarity and purpose. His approach is grounded in real-world experience, personal reflection, and the wisdom of numerous mentors who have shaped his thinking and leadership journey. Their influence—together with his own firsthand experiences—form the principles behind *Core Humility*.

Kevin is recognized for his approachable style and his commitment to helping others grow. Whether coaching one-on-one, facilitating leadership workshops, or speaking to larger audiences, he brings a calm, grounded energy that invites reflection and inspires action.

When he's not contributing to strategic initiatives or mentoring others, Kevin enjoys time with his family, exploring the outdoors, and playing a competitive game of pickleball. He's also learning to play golf and enjoys running—even at his "relaxed" pace. He finds joy in healthy growth, connecting with others, and the lifelong pursuit of learning.

Kevin and his wife, Natalie, reside in Lake Stevens, Washington, in the home where they raised their five children—now all married—and enjoy spending time with their growing family, including five grandchildren (and counting).

Kevin holds a bachelor's degree in engineering from Brigham Young University and an MBA from Seattle University.

He continues to believe that leadership is less about being in charge and more about showing up with humility, presence, and purpose.

To learn more about the training workshop that complements this book, please visit:

https://authenturecoaching.com.

Acknowledgements:

Authoring this book has been a deeply personal and rewarding journey—one that would not have been possible without the encouragement, insight, and support of many remarkable people.

To the mentors who have shaped my thinking and inspired my leadership path—Ed Pinegar, Rod Brower, Guy Payne, and John Haarlow—I am grateful for your wisdom, your example, and the way you've led with both strength and humility. Your influence is woven throughout these pages.

To my wife, Natalie—thank you for being my greatest supporter, my sounding board, and my editor-in-chief. Your thoughtful feedback, patience, and encouragement have given this book its heart.

To our children and their spouses—Kristen and McKay Perkins, Ryan and Emily Lavering, Mark and Rachel Lavering, Sean and Annie Lavering, and Sarah and Aaron Luce—thank you for your love, your insight, and for challenging me to think more deeply. And to our growing crew of grandchildren—you are a daily reminder of what matters most.

To my parents, Gordon and Annette Lavering—thank you for your unwavering generosity throughout my life and the values you instilled in me. They have shaped who I am, and your lasting influence continues to guide me in every chapter of life. I'm grateful for the lessons God taught me through you—and for His generous plan for us.

Special thanks to Kristen Perkins, Sarah Luce, Rachel Lavering, McKay Perkins, Sean Lavering, and Meghan Bean for reviewing early drafts, offering honest feedback, challenging ideas, and helping shape the message of this book. Your perspectives have made it stronger and more real.

To Sarah Luce—thank you for your creative contributions, illustrations, and support in bringing this book to life through marketing and publishing. Your talent and dedication have been invaluable.

Finally, to the friends and leaders from whom I've had the privilege of receiving mentoring, coaching, and learning from—thank you for your strengthening influence and for inspiring the ideas behind *Core Humility*. This book is as much about your influence and journey as it is mine.

With deep gratitude,

Kevin Lavering